TEACHING WITH THE

HEART
IN MIND™

This book is dedicated to the memory of my abuelita Teresa, who taught me how to move forward and gave me her blessings when I did.

Para ti, abuelita Teresa.

Brisca Publishing

infobriscapublishing@gmail.com

ISBN: 978-1-7360620-0-5 (print)

ISBN: 978-1-7360620-1-2 (ebook)

Ordering Information:

Special discounts are available on quantity purchases by corporations, associations, and others. For details, contact infobriscapublishing@gmail.com

Some names and identifying details have been changed to protect the privacy of individuals.

TABLE _of_ CONTENTS

TEACHING WITH THE
HEART
IN MIND™

A COMPLETE EDUCATOR'S GUIDE TO
SOCIAL EMOTIONAL LEARNING

LOREA MARTINEZ PEREZ, PhD

FOREWORD BY YVETTE JACKSON, EdD

Foreword

Yvette Jackson, Ed.D.

In the midst of the current dark shadow caused by the trauma of the pandemic and racialized injustice in our society, there is a light that shines from the hope of millions of students longing now, more than ever, to be intellectually and socially engaged so they can be inspired to actively participate in learning and strive for personal success. Unfortunately, thousands of teachers who have always worked valiantly to inspire these students have confided in me during our virtual professional learning sessions that stress from the daily uncertainty of how they will be delivering their teaching has assaulted their confidence. They feel unable to rise to the level of innovation needed to engage their students during the incessant trauma they are experiencing. Their diminishing confidence has seismic effect on their students, since students' mindsets and successes are not only based on their teachers' belief in their innate capacity for high levels of learning and intellectual performances, but also on the teachers' belief in their own ability to elicit and engage this capacity. These teachers ardently want to demonstrate their belief in the capacity and desire of their students for high levels of learning by providing rigorous and stimulating high-level strategies, but they poignantly realize that the negative emotions their students are experiencing dramatically distract and affect their learning. Their realization is substantiated by the neuroscience research that has demon-strated that although the brain, unlike the mind, is a biological entity and not a social or cultural product, the responses of the mind to experiences are emotional and effect the functioning of the brain. Emotional responses to positive experiences can trigger neurotransmitters which facilitate intel-lectual development, learning, creativity, resilience and confidence, while negative and traumatic experiences trigger neuro-inhibitors which depress these factors as well as "on your feet thinking".

The impact of the trauma of the current reality students and teachers are experiencing causes unrequited relationships that leave both students and teachers demotivated, disheartened and disengaged. Teachers are searching for strategies that will help them address the impact the trauma is having on students, hoping to also mitigate for its influence on themselves by boosting their resilience, thereby boosting their confidence. They want to not only provide innovative strategies to engage their students in academic learning, they also want to empower them with the social and emotional skills that enable them to cope with stress and trauma as well as develop the dispositions that enable them to strive and succeed. As Daniel Goleman elucidates so well, academic achievement might open doors for students, but it's the social and emotional skills that prepare them to thrive, flourish and lead in their endeavors for personal success.

Teaching with the HEART in Mind is the profound, exemplary guid-ing light for social-emotional learning and teaching! It provides educators with what they have expressed is so critically needed both now and in the immediate future as we consider vital ways to truly educate all our students for high levels of learning for self-actualization and self-transcendence: self-actualization that enables them to thrive in school and society, and self-transcendence that motivates them to contribute to that society.

Lorea's recounting of her personal experiences weave scholarship, em-pirical, cognitive and neuroscience research into an accessible, well-crafted narrative. This narrative substantiates the clearly articulated strategies she presents for social-emotional skill development for students and teachers; strategies that are designed to be delivered virtually or in school; strategies that boost the confidence of teachers to address the light of hope of our stu-dents to be engaged intellectually and socially so their brilliance can shine!

Introduction

Christine was a fifth-grade teacher in a disadvantaged community in East Oakland, California. She was on the quieter side, but when she spoke, all the other teachers listened. She had a strong commitment to serving and uplifting her students. "I have been teaching for six years in this community and I can tell you one thing—we won't be able to help these kids until we believe that they can and will learn and until students feel seen and loved," she told me one afternoon when I visited her classroom. It was no coincidence that Christine had great relationships with students. It was by design.

Students in Christine's class sat on the carpet every morning, forming a circle to share a favorite activity, discuss current events, or problem-solve a classroom conflict. She had a social-skills group during lunchtime and often played soccer with students after school. Relationships were at the heart of Christine's teaching, and she saw her interactions with students as the on/off switch to learning.

A new student came to Christine's class in the middle of the school year. Xavier's family had moved several times, and by the fifth grade he had attended seven different schools. Christine welcomed him and designated a couple of students to be his mentors until he felt comfortable; but Xavier wanted nothing to do with the mentor students and refused to do most of the class-work. Christine tried different strategies—having lunch with him, inviting him to be her helper, offering choices for completing his work, meeting with his family—but nothing seemed to work. Feeling defeated, Christine started to question whether she would be able to reach him. Given that Xavier would be moving on to middle school at the end of the year, Christine felt a sense of urgency. If she gave up, what would happen to him?

The school year ended and Xavier graduated. Christine didn't know anything more about him until the following year when he stopped by to visit. He told Christine that he liked his middle school and was doing well with his classes. And he told her that there was one thing he remembered from his time in her class—how she treated him like the other students, even when he was having a hard time.

Although Christine believed in the power of relationships, she'd thought her tools hadn't worked with Xavier. She was mistaken. Her words and actions—and the time she and Xavier had spent together—had a positive impact.

As educators, we plant seeds to develop our students' academic, social, and emotional capacity. Even though we may not see the fruit of our efforts until years later, teachers have the ability to nurture caring and supportive relationships that empower students to be their best selves; but they need to do the work. We have a big responsibility to grow caring, curious, and committed citizens who can go out into the world and make it a better place for all of humankind. We cannot do this without educating our students' hearts as well as their minds and we cannot wait for somebody else to do it; our students' future is at stake.

A path to grow hearts in our schools

After more than a decade teaching neurodiverse students, supporting teachers, and helping schools close the opportunity gap for students living in disadvantaged conditions, I realized that focusing solely on academics and standardized assessments was not going to change the odds for students. We needed to do something different to reach the whole child, build students' resilience, and spark their curiosity for learning. This is how I came to Social Emotional Learning (SEL), a field that has grown exponentially since I started researching it for my doctoral program in 2006.

In my doctoral dissertation, I investigated how teachers' practices changed over time as they implemented SEL lessons and practices. My findings revealed the positive impact this work can have, not only on teaching, but also on the social and emotional capacity of our educators.[1] This impactful research—and the positive transformation that I experienced in my own teaching—brought me to focus my life's work on SEL with the goal of helping people grow, lead, and teach with their hearts.

WHAT IS SEL?

"Social and emotional learning (SEL) is the process through which all young people and adults acquire and apply the knowledge, skills, and attitudes to develop healthy identities, manage emotions and achieve personal and collective goals, feel and show empathy for others, establish and maintain supportive relationships, and make responsible and caring decisions."[2]

—*The Collaborative for Academic, Social, and Emotional Learning (CASEL)*

Today, there is a broad consensus among educators and parents that education should go beyond teaching mathematics, language, and sciences to incorporate the development of social and emotional competencies—self-awareness, self-management, social awareness, relationship skills, responsible decision-making—that will support students in navigating an increasingly complex world with confidence, compassion, and success. In fact, 90 percent of teachers and school leaders show strong support for focusing on SEL in schools.[3]

As the world has been shaken by the novel coronavirus, COVID-19, and many people—including myself—have lost loved ones, faced job and food insecurity, or have been challenged by staying home 24/7, the need to support our students' social and emotional capacity has become even greater. The global pandemic has disproportionately impacted Black, Indigenous, and People of Color (BIPOC), and persons with disabilities, bringing to light the persistent systemic inequities in the US income, education, and health infrastructures.

In the transition from reactive to proactive actions during the pandemic, schools have quickly turned to SEL to guide efforts to support student mental health, engagement, and resilience. SEL has become an essential tool to "school community preparedness and the promotion of conditions for a thriving society."[4]

SEL is the vehicle that supports academic excellence, sustainable well-being, and committed citizenship. These social and emotional competencies not only help students pay attention in class or work collaboratively in a group project, they are also essential in the workplace and provide a road map for growth and life satisfaction into adulthood. By teaching these competencies to young people, we are planting the seeds for creating a more just, caring, and equitable future.

SEL impacts academic outcomes

Creating an SEL-rich learning community has significant behavior and academic outcomes for students. In a meta-analysis of 213 SEL programs, researchers found that students who participated in evidence-based SEL programs increased their positive social behaviors and had fewer conduct problems, less emotional distress, and improved academic performance.[5] These students also had improved attitudes toward self and others, and an increased connection to learning and schools. A 2015 publication from the Organization for Economic Co-operation and Development (OECD), *The Power of Social and Emotional Skills*, highlights the common set of skills that matter across cultures (including self-esteem, self-efficacy, and sociability).[6] These skills were shown to consistently affect outcomes like college completion, job attainment, health, and civic engagement. Although for many educators these research findings may not be surprising, it is encouraging to see the large amount of research that today supports the impact of SEL.

SEL means understanding our emotions

When we teach and learn SEL, we are building individuals' capacity to integrate their thoughts, emotions, and behaviors to accomplish important tasks in daily life.[7] We know from the latest research in neuroscience that emotions are an integral part of the brain's processes; in a way, by teaching SEL we are helping students use *all* the tools they already have, so they can pursue and accomplish professional and personal goals.

Emotions are involved in all major cognitive processes and serve several purposes. For instance, they:

- Protect us from dangerous situations by firing up our internal alarm system
- Help us make decisions by appraising different perspectives
- Support effective communication by creating a connection with other people
- Serve as a motivator to take action

Emotions also have a well-being purpose, allowing the individual to experience and enjoy small and big moments in life and accomplish goals. In fact, Dr. Susan David, renowned psychologist and author of *Emotional Agility*, argues that the way we navigate our inner worlds—what she defines as our everyday thoughts, emotions, and self-stories—is *the* single most important determinant of our life success.[8] People who are emotionally agile also deal with setbacks and struggles, but they know how to gain critical insight about situations from their feelings and how to use this knowledge to adapt, align their values, and make changes to bring the best of themselves forward.

SEL entails teaching these individual, learnable social and emotional competencies—such as being able to name and process our feelings, solve a conflict with a friend, understand the perspectives of others, and develop ways to positively contribute to the world—which can be developed over time through explicit instruction and supportive learning environments.

SEL is a reciprocal process

Did you notice that CASEL includes *adults* in their definition of SEL? This is because the work that needs to be done doesn't only apply to students. *The social and emotional competencies of the adults in the building matter*. And they matter a lot.

In a CASEL report that collected lessons learned from six years of systematic SEL implementation in some of the largest urban school districts in the United States, researchers found that SEL initiatives were more successful when schools had considered teachers' own social and emotional competencies.[9] Social and emotional competencies among educators improves teaching and learning by:

- Strengthening relationships among teachers and between students and teachers

- Reducing staff burnout, as teachers are able to incorporate tools to manage the stress that comes from teaching

- Building trust among colleagues

In addition, teachers model these social and emotional competencies to students whether consciously or not. For example, consider what happens if something has angered you and you say something harsh in the classroom—students learn from this behavior. They may think, "When I am upset, it is okay to express it by saying something hurtful." You shouldn't ignore or suppress your emotions in the classroom, in fact, I recommend that you share your feelings with your students. You can model *what to do* when you are experiencing strong emotions, and there is no better time for teachers to do this than when you are in that situation. In part three of this book, "The Whole-Hearted Educator," I go into depth about how teachers can cultivate their social and emotional capacity to find their voice, build resilience, and create a life with purpose.

SEL impacts conditions for learning

In addition to developing individual competencies, *SEL also considers the social and emotional conditions that affect learning and the classroom and school climate.* For example, the leadership and management style of school administrators and staff impacts the type of learning environment that is created in schools. When principals are warm toward students and approachable for families, they will more likely feel welcome in the school. At the same time, the rules and protocols that schools put into place to address students' misbehavior will influence the learning environment that is created at school. For instance, restorative justice focuses on building relationships and repairing harm rather than simply punishing students for misbehavior. In schools that incorporate restorative practices, when people make mistakes or cause harm, restorative interventions help these students or adults understand the impact of their actions, heal the harm, and restore the community. These conditions for learning affect students' attendance, motivation, academic learning, social and emotional capacity, and well-being.

Some schools and districts focus on the *teaching* of social and emotional competencies as the first step in their SEL implementation efforts, but SEL is more than just a program or lesson; it is about considering how your school policies and your teacher practices support (or fail to support) students' learning and growth, and making appropriate changes when needed.

Imagine a middle school student, Shakti, who doesn't participate in whole class conversations. She may feel insecure, shy, or afraid to make a mistake. The teacher could focus on teaching Shakti strategies to manage her emotions in these situations. That would be helpful. However, in addition to teaching these management tools, the teacher could also consider adapting her teaching to better meet Shakti's needs. For example, by providing the question ahead of the classroom conversation, so Shakti can prepare a response, or by creating opportunities for her to participate in smaller group conversations that increase in size over time. The key here is to consider not only the skills that students should develop (and that we will teach) but also how our teaching practices may impact students' ability to engage with the content, engage with their peers, and learn what they need to learn. In Chapter Four, "Developing Positive Conditions for Learning," I explore the four building blocks to creating a safe and supportive learning environment.

SEL removes and mitigates barriers to learning

As much as SEL is a process for teaching social and emotional competencies to students, it is also a schoolwide effort to remove barriers to learning. This happens when all of the stakeholders in the school community are involved: administrators, educators (including those outside of school), students, families, and community partners. These partnerships not only enrich students' experiences in school, they also provide a sense that everybody is working together to support students' learning and growth.

TEACHING WITH THE HEART IN MIND

In my work helping schools with SEL implementation, I found myself pulling elements from different frameworks in order to fully support the needs of learners and educators. While certain frameworks provide a list of clearly defined competencies, many lack a scope and sequence with specific goals by grade level or age range, which makes planning effective lessons more difficult. In other cases, the framework does illustrate how competencies develop over time, but it lacks cultural sensitivity. As much as I wanted to stick with one model—it would have made my life easier!—I realized I had to create something that would overcome some of the challenges I had encountered in other models. It would also need to incorporate my experience in the classroom and as an SEL consultant, supporting teachers in developing their own social and emotional capacity. This is why Teaching with the HEART in Mind was born.

Teaching with the HEART in Mind provides the kind of practical guidance I wish I'd had when I was a classroom teacher. It is grounded in research, input from experts in the field, and the teaching and consulting experiences I have had over the years. With this book, based on the latest research on how the brain works, you will learn *why* we cannot separate SEL from effective teaching; *what* we need to teach in order to support our students' academic, social, and emotional growth; and *how* to create caring and supportive classroom communities where students can reach their full potential.

But remember this work is not just about the kids, it's also about the adults; educators cannot effectively teach what they don't understand, practice, and model. Only when adults make sense of their own emotional intelligence can they remove the social and emotional barriers that hinder students' ability to learn and achieve. Therefore, educators also need support to nurture their own well-being and learn tools to navigate the unprecedented challenges of teaching during and after a pandemic. Teaching with the HEART in Mind is a framework that will help you develop your emotional intelligence, resilience, and well-being and transform your teaching practice.

The HEART in Mind model represents a practical application of essential knowledge, attitudes, and skills for students and adults to be socially, emotionally, and culturally competent in their lives. It incorporates *intrapersonal skills*, such as self-awareness and self-management; *interpersonal skills,* such as social awareness and relationship building; and *cognitive skills*, such as ethical decision-making. These important skills are represented by the acronym HEART and are organized to show you a developmentally appropriate progression of skill development. In addition, these skills are described using a *verb* to indicate a specific action, something we can do to put that skill into practice.

The HEART in Mind Model

Intrapersonal Skills	**H**	Honor Your Emotions	Naming, interpreting, and appropriately communicating feelings
	E	Elect Your Responses	Creating space to make constructive and safe decisions
Interpersonal Skills	**A**	Apply Empathy	Recognizing and valuing the emotions and perspectives of others and taking action to support them. Nurturing self-compassion
	R	Reignite Your Relationships	Nurturing a positive and supportive network by actively using communication and conflict-resolution skills and working cooperatively with diverse individuals and groups
Cognitive Skills	**T**	Transform with Purpose	Using personal assets and interests to positively contribute to self and others

Although this book is written mainly for teachers who want to teach and integrate SEL practices in their schools and classrooms, these skills are just as important in the life of a teacher, a school administrator, or a parent. The expectations we would have for a seven-year-old student will be different, but the skills themselves are relevant for students and adults alike.

Because the tools in this book are universal, they can be easily adapted across PreK-12 and in multiple settings. Whether you are concerned with a preschooler who yells when he is upset, a third grader who cannot focus in class, or a middle schooler who feels lonely, you can find supportive practices here that will help you to understand, consider your options, and act on these situations from a place of caring, courage, and confidence.

The HEART in Mind model is not a "plug and play" tool, but a process to help educators create social and emotional conditions to support engaged and purposeful learners in the virtual or physical classroom. While teaching HEART skills to students is part of this process, SEL is most effective when these skills are infused into the curriculum and integrated into the course of the day, and when educators practice and model these skills.

In summary, teaching with the HEART in Mind means:

- Developing positive conditions for learning

- Teaching and integrating the HEART in Mind model in your classroom

- Nurturing your own social and emotional capacity to become a whole-hearted educator

Think about teaching with the HEART in Mind not as a destination or a final outcome, but as a vehicle for learning, growing, and creating a better future with and for your students.

About this book

In this three-part book, you will learn practical ways to model and teach HEART skills, infuse them into your teaching, and create a relationship-centered classroom conducive to meaningful and purposeful learning.

Part one provides foundational background information. This is the *why*. Chapters One through Three are an overview of the research and theories linking SEL with academic and life outcomes and its connections with the science of learning and development. Each chapter has strategies for applying these research findings in the classroom.

Part two contains information and exercises for implementing the HEART in Mind model in your classroom, including strategies for virtual settings. This is the *what* and the *how* for classrooms: what skills need to be taught and how to infuse them in the classroom to create a positive environment. Chapter Four includes strategies for creating appropriate social and emotional conditions conducive to learning; Chapter Five and Six provide an in-depth exploration of the five HEART skills with specific activities and tools for classroom application, including tips for integrating this model into the virtual classroom; Chapter Seven includes a process for reviewing lesson plans through an SEL lens. Students will benefit most if you implement these tools routinely, not as a one-time event.

Part three provides information about the importance of adult social and emotional capacity. This is the *what* and *how* for educators. Chapters Seven through Nine contain practical strategies for facilitating with the HEART in mind effectively, developing resilience, and connecting teaching with an overall sense of purpose. While it may be tempting to skip this section, you are an important part of this process. When educators are able to be patient and compassionate with themselves, and have strategies to reduce their stress, they are more likely to be present and available for their students.

The time is now to educate the hearts and minds of our students and the adults who work with them. We have the power to create healing communities where children, youth, and adults can thrive. Let's get started on your journey to teach with the HEART in Mind!

Teaching with the *HEART in Mind*™

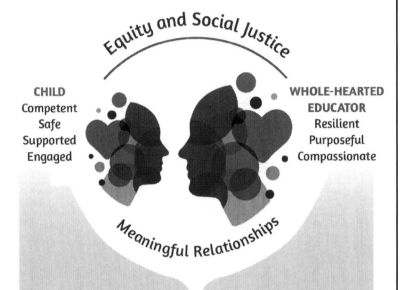

Equity and Social Justice

CHILD
Competent
Safe
Supported
Engaged

WHOLE-HEARTED EDUCATOR
Resilient
Purposeful
Compassionate

Meaningful Relationships

I am socially, emotionally, and culturally competent.

I feel physically, emotionally, and intellectually safe, and am treated equitably.

I experience challenging and engaging instruction.

I feel supported and connected to the world around me.

I teach and practice HEART skills, resilience and shared ownership in my classroom.

I provide behavioral supports, create healthy boundaries, and identity safe spaces.

I center my instruction on my students with high expectations and academic mindsets.

I nurture meaningful connections and belonging, and provide effective supports.

└────── Social and Emotional Conditions for Learning ──────┘

HEART Skills

Honor Your Emotions

Elect Your Responses

Apply Empathy

Reignite Your Relationships

Transform with Purpose

Endnotes

1   Martínez, Lorea. "Teachers' Voices on Social Emotional Learning: Identifying the conditions that make implementation possible." PhD diss., Universitat Autònoma de Barcelona, 2013, http://hdl.handle.net/10803/378029.

2   Collaborative for Academic, Social, and Emotional Learning (CASEL). "What is SEL?" CASEL website. Access October 14, 2020, www.casel.org/what-is-sel/.

3   Bridgeland, John, Mary Bruce, and Arya Hariharan. "The Missing Piece: A National Teacher Survey on How Social and Emotional Learning Can Empower Children and Transform Schools." Collaborative for Academic, Social, and Emotional Learning (CASEL). Accessed September 18, 2020, https://casel.org/wp-content/uploads/2016/01/the-missing-piece.pdf.

4   Cipriano, Christina, Gabrielle Rappolt-Schlichtmann, and Marc Brackett. "Supporting School Community Wellness with Social and Emotional Learning (SEL) During and After a Pandemic." PennState College of Health and Human Development. August 2020. https://www.prevention.psu.edu/uploads/files/PSU-SEL-Crisis-Brief.pdf.

5   Durlak, Joseph A., Roger P. Weissberg, Alison B. Dymnicki, Rebecca D. Taylor, and Kristen B. Schellinger. "The Impact of Enhancing Students' Social and Emotional Learning: A Meta-Analysis of School-Based Universal Interventions." *Child Development* 82, no. 1 (January/February 2011): 405–432. https://casel.org/wp-content/uploads/2016/06/meta-analysis-child-development-1.pdf

6   OECD, ed. *Skills for Social Progress: The Power of Social and Emotional Skills*. Paris: OECD Publishing, 2015. https://doi.org/10.1787/9789264226159-en.

7   Zins, Joseph, Roger P. Weissberg, Margaret C. Wang, and Herbert J. Walberg, eds. *Building Academic Success on Social and Emotional Learning: What Does the Research Say?* New York: Teachers College Press, 2014.

8   David, Susan. *Emotional Agility: Get Unstuck, Embrace Change, and Thrive in Work and Life.* New York: Avery, 2016.

9   Collaborative for Academic, Social, and Emotional Learning (CASEL), ed. "Key Implementation Insights from the Collaborating Districts Initiative." June 2017. https://www.casel.org/wp-content/uploads/2017/06/CDI-Insights-Report-May.pdf.

PART 1: LEARNING IS SOCIAL, EMOTIONAL, AND ACADEMIC

Chapter 1: We Feel, Therefore We Learn

Ms. Perkins, a first-grade classroom teacher, greets her students at the door every morning. She says the student's name, makes eye contact, and waits for students to choose a nonverbal greeting: they can give her a hug or a high five. When it is Sheila's turn, Ms. Perkins can see that something is wrong. Sheila has her head down. She's looking at her feet and moving slowly toward her.

"Good morning, Ms. Sheila. What's the matter?" asks Ms. Perkins. Sheila tries to move past, but Ms. Perkins softly touches her shoulder and kneels to make eye contact. "I can see things aren't quite right this morning. Do you need a hug or a high five?" Sheila gives Ms. Perkins a hug, and the teacher, hugging her back, says, "We are going to have a great day today."

Sheila enters the classroom and joins her classmates on the carpet. It's time for morning meeting. During this time, students sing a classroom song, play a quick group game, and count how many students are present that day. Then they sit down on the carpet as Ms. Perkins begins reviewing the day's schedule.

Emotions are an important part of human life and they greatly influence students' readiness for learning. If you are an educator, you know that the first few minutes of class can be chaotic and a difficult transition for some students. Students might be distressed about parents' constant fights, excited to see their friends, or worried about presenting a classroom project. The sadness or stress Sheila was experiencing that morning would probably make it difficult for her to focus on academic content unless she had an opportunity to manage these feelings. Ms. Perkins' initial conversation with Sheila, and the morning meeting that followed, are two great strategies for identifying how students are feeling and supporting their transition from home to the classroom.

Many teachers know that greeting students at the door helps to start the day with a positive tone. It is an opportunity for students and teachers to acknowledge each other, and a chance for the teacher to do an informal assessment of the classroom's general *mood*. Are students particularly energetic or tired? Are there students having a difficult morning? This is valuable information that the teacher can use in her instruction by slightly tweaking the morning schedule, switching student groups, or giving additional attention to a particular student.

Having a morning meeting helps in building a community in which students have a sense of safety and belonging, even when you cannot be physically together. Most of these meetings are focused on building trust and making sure that every student in the classroom feels seen and heard. Morning meetings are also a place where the important social and emotional competencies—which we will call HEART skills, following the HEART in Mind model—required for students' academic success and personal well-being can be explicitly taught.

After decades of research and practice, we know that these social and emotional competencies improve academic and life outcomes.[10] When schools teach and model them, motivation to learn increases, problem behaviors decrease, and test scores go up.[11] In a way, research into Social Emotional Learning—the process of developing intrapersonal, interpersonal, and cognitive skills that are vital for school, work, and life success—has proven what many educators knew all along: students learn more and better when they are socially and emotionally capable, supported by caring adults, and they feel safe in school.

In recent years, new knowledge about human development—from neuroscience and the science of learning and development—has demonstrated that emotions and social relationships strongly influence learning.[12] In fact, affective neuroscientist and human-development psychologist, Dr. Mary Helen Immordino-Yang, has found that it is *neurobiologically impossible* to build memories, engage complex thoughts, or make meaningful decisions without emotion.[13] As you can imagine, these findings have huge implications for teaching and learning! In this chapter, we will learn more about the role that emotions play in learning, and how we can apply these findings in the classroom.

HOW EMOTIONS AFFECT LEARNING

"Learning is dynamic, social, and context-dependent because emotions are, and emotions form a critical piece of how, what, when, and why people think, remember, and learn."

—*Dr. Immordino-Yang*

We experience emotions all the time: frustrated that the neighbor blasts loud music at 5:30 a.m., worried about a sick relative, or overwhelmed by unpaid bills. We often experience several of these emotions at the same time! Emotions drive our attention; they influence our ability to process information and understand what we encounter. They can energize our thinking or distract us from our goals. In short, we need our emotions for thinking, problem-solving, and decision-making.

Neuroscience has shown that common actions for students in school, such as decoding a word or doing a science experiment, are experienced subjectively and evaluated emotionally in terms of a person's predispositions and memories, even though they may be unaware of these feelings. Traditionally, in the West, emotions were considered interferences in the learning process, so students were often told to leave their emotions at the door and just focus on academic work.

Research has revealed that emotions are not add-ons, distinct from cognitive skills. Today we know that cognition and emotion are supported by interdependent neural processes: you cannot have thoughts without feeling, and vice versa. Dr. Immordino-Yang argues that even in academic subjects traditionally considered unemotional, such as physics or engineering, deep understanding depends on making emotional connections between concepts. For example, when students are solving equations and they perceive them as "beautiful" instead of "ugly," they activate the emotional region in their brains, which is necessary for developing intrinsically motivated learning.

Many educators have had students who ask, "Why are we doing this?" when presented with new information, or others who say, "Are we doing this *again*?" Well, there is a scientific reason for these questions. The brain does not waste energy thinking about things that don't matter to us. *We only think deeply about things we care about.* This is the reason why learners—both children and adults—pay attention and stay focused when the subjects or topics discussed in class are *personally relevant* to them.

Unfortunately, teachers often resort to saying things like, "This unit is going to be on the test," to draw students' attention to the content discussed in class. Students may have no internal reason to engage with that information, but they do it, nonetheless, for another emotion-related reason: fear. They may be afraid of failing that class, disappointing their families, or feeling ashamed. Dr. Immordino-Yang argues, however, that fear shifts one's thought patterns and memory, putting students in a fight-or-flight response, which is not conducive to deep engagement with ideas or skill development.[14] Students' learning is impaired when they are fearful, traumatized, or overcome by challenging emotions.

On the other hand, curiosity is a much better emotion for meaningful learning. Curiosity fuels imagination and creativity. When students feel curious, they are open; they may feel intellectually playful and willing to explore new possibilities. Great innovators, such as Thomas Edison or Leonardo da Vinci, have curious minds. For educators focused on creating productive learning environments, this means that we need to find more effective tools to increase curiosity. We need more "emotional hooks" to induce emotions that support deeper learning in the classroom. (You will find practical examples demonstrating emotional hooks in Chapter Five).

SO, WHAT ARE EMOTIONS?

Emotions are complex states of mind and body that are generally activated by an event known as a *stimulus*. Events can be external (you received great news from a friend) or internal (you have a toothache); they can also be real (your spouse was in a car accident) or imagined (you get excited when thinking about the weekend). Once a stimulus has been generated, there is a process to *appraise* it.[15] This process is automatic and determines whether the event is perceived as positive or negative, which will produce an emotional response. For example, if you are riding your bike and a car gets too close, you will probably appraise that you are in danger. This will activate an emotional response. We can identify three different emotional responses:[16]

1. Physiological: involuntary responses such as sweat, dry mouth, heavy breathing, or rapid heartbeat

2. Behavioral: facial expressions, body language, or tone of voice

3. Cognitive: the subjective experience of the emotion. This allows us to become aware and name our emotions. Having the language to name and describe our emotions is key to identifying what's happening.

Although emotions involve automatic mental and physical reactions to different situations, not everybody reacts the same way. Some people are more reactive—or react differently—than others. The early childhood years are the most critical in establishing the neural connections that provide the foundation for emotional health and social skills such as language, reasoning, and problem solving, among others.[17] When students experience trauma or recurrent stress at a young age as a result of their living situation and/or the impact of generational issues such as racism, oppression, or inequality, their nervous system and their abilities to regulate emotion are impacted.

At the same time, dominant cultural and social norms in the United States promote negative biases and stereotypes about Black, Indigenous, and People of Color (BIPOC), and individuals from low-income backgrounds.[18] Experiences of racism and discrimination negatively impact students as they try to cope with racialized stress and micro-aggressions. Moreover, BIPOC students are disciplined in schools at higher rates than their White counterparts, which in turn impacts those students' academic, social, and emotional growth.[19]

In order to understand students' emotional lives, we need to understand the larger sociopolitical context, which according to Dr. Dena Simmons, assistant director of the Yale Center for Emotional Intelligence, "is fraught with injustice and inequity and affects our students' lives."[20] As educators teaching with the HEART in Mind, we need to develop cultural awareness of our learned beliefs and how the stereotypes and prejudices we hold about students—specially BIPOC students—can impact our SEL understanding and practice.

Emotions are not static; they are temporary states, but they develop with maturity and experience. Imagine a student, Kian, starting fifth grade in a new school. How do you think he feels: nervous, worried, maybe timid? Now picture Kian at the end of the school year—he is feeling joyful, relaxed, and proud of everything he accomplished that year. How do you think Kian's emotions might influence his ability to take on future challenges? Research shows that emotions guide people's perceptions of the world and their memories of the past. Kian's challenging experience of starting in a new school is now associated in his memory with positive emotions.

Positive psychologist Barbara L. Fredrickson defines positive emotions as *pleasant affective states* such as joy, gratitude, serenity, interest, hope, or love. In her research, Fredrickson found that positive emotions broaden people's awareness in ways that, over time, incrementally build their resources and resilience.[21] This doesn't mean that educators should focus on making students feel *happy* at all times; however, students should experience a broad range of pleasant emotions—such as curiosity, interest, or excitement—in the classroom, so that they become more invested in their learning outcomes.

Consider a fourth grader, Maya, who incorrectly solves a math problem in front of her classmates and is sent back to her seat. She feels ashamed and tells herself, "I can't do math. Why did I volunteer to solve that problem? I am stupid." Maya's emotional reaction to the outcome of this situation—feeling ashamed and having negative self-talk—will consciously or unconsciously shape her future behavior, probably by avoiding a similar situation. Dr. Immordino-Yang explains that learners' emotional reactions to the outcomes of their choices become implicitly attached to the cognitive knowledge about that domain—in this case, solving math problems or volunteering in math class. That is to say, for Maya, solving math problems in front of her classmates (or even solving math problems alone) is no longer a "neutral" experience. *Students' emotional learning shapes their future behavior.*

Emotions drive us to take action, either by facing an event or by moving away from the situation that produced the emotions. This predisposition to action is also known as the fight-flight-freeze response, which reflects basic behaviors that ensure survival. When children, youth, or adults experience "big" emotions—such as anger or fear—our amygdala (the "fire alarm" in the limbic system, which activates a set of responses meant to promote survival) may interpret it as *danger*, sending adrenaline into our bodies to cope with the perceived danger.

During these situations of "amygdala hijacking," as psychologist Dr. Daniel Goleman calls them, the stressors that are generated in our bodies override the rational parts of the brain—specifically, the prefrontal cortex. The prefrontal cortex is the executive processing area of the brain: it helps us to pay attention, control our impulses, solve problems, or make appropriate decisions. When a child's emotions take over, she may hit a classmate during a competitive game during recess or say hurtful words to a friend during a disagreement. Although students may regret their actions later, during those emotionally charged situations they are being reactive to "protect" themselves from the perceived danger.

When the amygdala works properly, it is a great protective system: if a tiger is chasing you, you need to run! However, in our contemporary times, people's nervous systems are triggered unnecessarily by events that are hardly life-threatening. A significant increase in the stress levels amongst

Americans[22] indicates that our brains are *frequently* responding to everyday events with a fight-flight-freeze response. Based on these data, scholars have started referring to Generation X (those born between the early 1960s and early 1980s) and millennials (those born between 1981 and 1996) as "Generation Stress."[23]

When people experience stress responses frequently, they don't go back to a normal (calm) state as easily; their baseline shifts, hovering much closer to a near-constant survival response. They might often feel impulsive, overwhelmed, and reactive. Their ability to access their prefrontal cortex gets diminished, which means that thinking clearly or being attentive to others becomes increasingly difficult. When individuals are repeatedly exposed to many different stressors for an extended period of time, they may develop chronic stress, which can seriously impact their physical and emotional health.

Children and youth may experience stress due to large stressors (such as home violence) or small ones (such as being worried about a math test). Students may also experience stress from threats to emotional safety and feelings of belonging. Although the magnitude of these stressors is quite different, the stress response experienced by the child is the same. And here's the thing: when students are too stressed, they cannot learn. The brain does not focus or remember information well under stress: stress affects students' neural functioning, robbing them of working-memory resources.[24]

The negative effects of stress, however, can be buffered through supportive parenting, relationships, community, and school programs. So, today it is even more important for families and educators to pay attention to the *conditions* for learning taking place in our schools and homes. Are young people's social and emotional development being supported? Is their well-being prioritized? If the answer is no, let's get to work.

OUR EMOTIONAL LIVES

Emotions are an important part of being human. We don't want to ignore or suppress them because they provide valuable data about what is happening inside ourselves and the world around us. Sharon Salzberg, world-renowned meditation teacher and *New York Times* bestselling author, explains how we are conditioned to believe that painful feelings are "bad" and pleasurable ones are "good." For many people, it's often easier to avoid grief and sorrow, while only embracing pleasant sensations like confidence or love.[25] SEL means developing our capacity to accept and embrace *all* emotions, including the unpleasant ones, so that we can experience a more enduring sense of happiness and life satisfaction.

Students bring emotions from life outside of school to the classroom; they might be dealing with an ongoing stressful situation at home, like a divorce or a parent losing their job, or maybe something more momentary, like an argument with a sibling. If students don't have a chance to regulate their emotions before getting to school, they will need support to cool off and refocus before they can move on with their day. In Sheila's story at the beginning of the chapter, you read how the personal connection with the teacher and the morning meeting supported students' transitions from home to the classroom, honoring the reality that students may come to school in different emotional states.

In addition, students also experience emotions that originate *in* the classroom, even in a distance-learning environment. According to educational psychologist Dr. Reinhard Pekrun, there are four groups of academic emotions especially relevant for students' learning:[26]

1. *Achievement emotions* relate to success and failure resulting from classroom activities. Students might feel hope and pride when they have been successful, but they can also feel anxiety, shame, or fear of failure. Taking tests, for example, tends to create high levels of anxiety and stress in our students.

2. *Epistemic emotions* are emotions triggered by cognitive problems. For example, feeling surprised when a new task is presented in class, frustrated about an obstacle with the science project, or delighted when a math problem is successfully solved. These are especially important in learning new, non-routine tasks.

3. *Topic emotions* pertain to the topics/subjects presented in class. Students might feel excited about a new art class, disgusted with certain lab experiments, or saddened by the fate of a character in a novel.

4. *Social emotions* relate to teachers and classmates as students and teachers work together and interact in the classroom. Compassion, envy, sympathy, anger, or social anxiety can be present at different times during the day with any and all of our students.

As a teacher, it might be difficult (almost impossible!) to respond to your students' emotions at all times while you manage the classroom and attend to academic content. However, it's critical for educators to understand the kinds of emotions students experience in the classroom, how such emotions differ among students, and how they influence students' engagement and performance.

It is also important for educators to consider how students' emotional lives impact their own feelings. Many times, educators go through a full teaching day without noticing how they feel, until something happens and they overreact over a small incident. Embracing SEL means that educators also explore their emotional lives so that they can increase their self-awareness and help students in doing the same.

During a training on how to incorporate SEL into teaching practices, a middle school foreign language teacher said, "There is no shame in my classroom. All students participate in class discussions and presentations without any problems." While the teacher's intent was to create a shame-free classroom, the reality is that students *may feel shame* speaking in a foreign language. As a result of having a better understanding of how emotions influence learning, this teacher started to do "check-in" activities with her students at the beginning and end of the class.

One of her favorites was to have students write on a Post-it note how they felt at the beginning and the end of the class. Although students probably felt additional emotions during that period, this *emotion map* gave the teacher insight into students' experiences. This check-in activity became her tool to check progress against her goal of creating a safe environment. At the same time, students started developing their self-awareness as they were asked and encouraged to check in with themselves and name their emotions.

As we have seen, emotions drive us to action, but that doesn't *necessarily* mean that we need to act based on our emotions! Our natural predisposition to reaction can be regulated with some training; this is where teaching

HEART skills comes into play, as with this middle school foreign language teacher who was enhancing students' ability to connect with themselves and name their emotions through a simple check-in routine. Students can't understand or navigate their inner experiences until they first become aware of what is going on inside. Once students have awareness of the emotions they feel, they will be more likely to interpret their feelings and make sense of their emotional life. The same is true for us educators.

When teachers are familiar with the critical role that emotions play in learning, they can use this knowledge to design educational experiences that incorporate emotions into teaching and learning, by considering their students' lived experiences and the diverse contexts students need to navigate. Here are a few ideas to get you started:

 Summary: The Role of Emotions in Learning

- Emotions drive attention, they influence our ability to process information and understand what we encounter.
- Cognition and emotion are supported by interdependent neural processes. You cannot have thoughts without feeling, and vice versa.
- We only think deeply about things we care about. The brain does not waste energy thinking about things that don't matter to us.
- Students' trauma and recurrent stress due to individual or social issues, such as racism, injustice, and discrimination impact their ability to express and regulate emotions.
- Emotions develop with maturity and experience. They guide people's perceptions of the world and their memories of the past.
- Positive emotions, such as curiosity, support meaningful learning; while other emotions, such as fear, only support compliance.
- The brain does not focus or remember information well under stress; stress affects students' neural functioning, robbing them of working-memory resources.
- Students' emotional experiences in class influence their engagement and performance.

STRATEGIES TO INCORPORATE EMOTIONS
IN THE CLASSROOM

Research in the field of neuroscience has demonstrated that emotions affect learning. Pleasant emotions, such as curiosity or interest, open up students' minds to learning. Feelings of fear or chronic stress hinder young people's readiness for the academic and social demands of the classroom. Educators have the potential to create safe and supportive learning environments that incorporate what we know about the role of emotions in learning. These are some strategies to make it happen:

- *Give students choices.* When students are involved in making decisions about (a) their research topic, (b) ways to complete a task, or (c) showing mastery of a standard, they will likely be more emotionally invested in and attached to the learning outcomes. This is not news for educators, right? Teachers know that choice, when provided in a structured manner, can motivate students and instill a sense of ownership over the learning process.

- *Help students relate the materials discussed in class to their life and personal interests.* Earlier, we discussed how the brain doesn't pay attention to things we don't care about. When students engage with academic material in a meaningful way, they will be able to pay more attention and focus for longer periods of time.

An easy way to get to know your students is to have them complete a personal inventory; have students write down the things they like to do, the things they do well, and things that might be hard or boring for them. Ask your students about different aspects of their lives, such as favorite school subjects, the sports and hobbies they enjoy, and their relationships and family. Creating these personal inventories will help students develop a better understanding of themselves.

As a teacher, you can use these inventories to get to know your students better and connect their interests to the materials discussed in the classroom. You may also consider displaying these inventories (or a section of them) in class, as a visual reminder that we all have strengths. These emotional connections will help students apply the content you teach in real-life situations, while developing their self-awareness.

- *Create opportunities to solve open-ended problems.* Dr. Immordino-Yang argues that highly prescriptive activities are emotionally impoverished. That is to say, they don't allow students to establish the emotional connections that are important for cognitive learning and decision-making. Instead, classroom activities should allow students' emotions to appear (comfortable or uncomfortable), along with opportunities for students to make mistakes and learn from them. Project-based learning, group work, or even classroom discussions about current events can be effective in letting students wrestle with problems that don't have a right/wrong solution.

- *Offer a variety of tasks and activities* and combine both achievement and performance tasks so students can feel successful during class. Building self-confidence in your students by providing opportunities for success and accomplishment is key to promoting a joy for learning and avoiding achievement anxiety.

- *Build in regular check-ins with students* (beginning, during, and/or at the end of the day/class). These can take the form of a classroom meeting but could also be a silent activity where students quickly share or write how they are feeling. You might also use check-in time to ask for feedback about lessons, classroom routines, or particular projects students are developing.

- *Create a space and/or provide time in the classroom to refocus.* This can be a calming corner, where students go to regulate their emotions and get ready to reengage with the classroom. You can also implement a scheduled quiet time, which provides students with a regular quiet and peaceful period to take a breath or perhaps do sustained silent reading or free drawing. The idea is to help students de-stress and refocus for better learning, acknowledging that a short time using one of these strategies can support sustained focus in the long term.

TAKEAWAYS AND NEXT STEPS

Find a pencil and a piece of paper and answer the following questions:

	Main Ideas What are the key takeaways for you from this chapter?
	Insights What did you think while you were reading? How did you feel? What surprised you?
	Direction What does this mean for your work as an educator? What one or two actions will you be taking to incorporate emotions into your teaching?

Endnotes

10   Durlak, Joseph A., Roger P. Weissberg, Alison B. Dymnicki, Rebecca D. Taylor, and Kristen B. Schellinger. "The Impact of Enhancing Students' Social and Emotional Learning: A Meta-Analysis of School-Based Universal Interventions." *Child Development* 82, no. 1 (January/February 2011): 405–432. https://casel.org/wp-content/uploads/2016/06/meta-analysis-child-development-1.pdf.

11   Jones, Stephanie M., and Jennifer Kahn. "The Evidence Base for How We Learn: Supporting Students' Social, Emotional, and Academic Development." The Aspen Institute. September 13, 2017.

12   Darling-Hammond, Linda, and Channa M. Cook-Harvey. "Educating the Whole Child: Improving School Climate to Support Student Success." Learning Policy Institute. September 2018.

13   Immordino-Yang, Mary Helen. *Emotions, Learning, and the Brain: Exploring the Educational Implications of Affective Neuroscience.* New York: W. W. Norton & Company, 2015.

14   Martínez, Lorea, and Susan Stillman, eds. *The EQ Educator: Taking Social Emotional Learning to Schools.* CA: Six Seconds, 2018.

15   Lazarus, R. S. "Progress on a cognitive-motivational-relational theory of emotion." *American Psychologist* 46, no. 8 (1991): 819–834.

16   Bisquerra Alzina, Rafael. *Psicopedagogía de las emociones.* Madrid: Síntesis, 2009.

17   Mason, Christine, Michele M. Rivers Murphy, and Yvette Jackson. *Mindfulness Practices: Cultivating Heart Centered Communities Where Students Focus and Flourish (Creating a Positive Learning Environment Through Mindfulness in Schools).* Bloomington: Solution Tree Press, 2018.

18   Ibid

19   Little, Shafiqua J., and Richard O. Welsh. "Rac(e)ing to punishment? Applying theory to racial disparities in disciplinary outcomes." *Race Ethnicity and Education* (April 2019). https://doi.org/10.1080/13613324.2019.1599344.

20   Simmons, Dena. "Why We Can't Afford Whitewashed Social Emotional Learning." *ASCD Education Update* 61, no. 4 (April 2019). http://www.ascd.org/publications/newsletters/education_update/apr19/vol61/num04/Why_We_Can't_Afford_Whitewashed_Social-Emotional_Learning.aspx.

21   Fredrickson, Barbara L. "Biological Underpinnings of Positive Emotions and Purpose." In *The Social Psychology of Living Well*, edited by Joseph P. Forgas and Roy F. Baumeister, 163–180. New York: Routledge, 2018.

22   "Stress in America." American Psychological Association. 2020. https://www.apa.org/news/press/releases/stress/index.aspx.

23   "Stress by Generation." American Psychological Association. 2012. https://www.apa.org/news/press/releases/stress/2012/generation.pdf.

24   Immordino-Yang, Mary Helen, Linda Darling-Hammond, and Christina Krone. *The Brain Basis for Integrated Social, Emotional, and Academic Development. How emotions and social relationships drive learning.* Washington, D.C.: The Aspen Institute, 2018.

25   Salzberg, Sharon. *Real Love. The Art of Mindful Connection.* New York: Flatiron Books, 2017.

26   Pekrun, Reinhard. *Emotions and Learning.* Burbank: The International Academy of Education, 2014.

Chapter 2: A Champion for Every Child

One of my first teaching assignments was in a public school in Barcelona. I met the principal and the dean of students on the afternoon before starting my new position and was told, "This is a very difficult group of students, some with challenging behaviors. Do you think you can do it?" I really wanted to teach at that school, so—although I had my doubts—I said, "Of course!" I didn't sleep at all that night; I was scared and felt unprepared.

The principal and dean hadn't lied; it was a challenging group of students. However, I was determined to make it work. I had several not-so-great teaching moments, but over time, the kids started to warm up to me and were excited to have me as their teacher.

There was one particular student who kept me up at night. He had tried to jump out of a moving car two years earlier and was receiving counseling from a therapist outside of school. It was difficult for me to predict his behavior in class; he could go from engaged and cooperative to defiant in seconds. The other students were always watching to see how I would respond to his behavior. It was stressful! My strategy with him was to keep a personal connection. Despite how difficult it was to deal with his outbursts, I tried to find small moments where we could relate to each other, sometimes over a soccer game, a TV series, or even a math problem.

A few weeks before the end of the school year, his therapist called me. Although this was a routine check-in call, I didn't know what to expect and felt nervous. When I answered the phone, the therapist started talking and I could feel my heart racing. I will never forget his words: "I don't know what you are doing, but it is working. I have never seen him so happy with school."

Nurturing that personal connection paid off over time. Although that student continued to display challenging behaviors in the classroom, his outbursts decreased. We established a positive understanding of each other and kept in touch even after the school year had ended.

Although I did not know it at the time, my experience with this student illustrates a key finding from the science of learning and development: children's relationships with adults are an essential ingredient for learning and healthy development.[27] The quality of teacher-student relationships has been repeatedly linked with students' academic, social, and emotional outcomes. More specifically, when positive and supportive student-teacher relationships exist in classrooms, students are more likely to use their teachers as resources to help solve problems, actively engage in learning activities, and better navigate the demands of school.[28]

What would you do if you knew you could decrease the likelihood of your students having substance-abuse problems, engaging in risky sex, or being arrested for severe violence and drug-related crimes? SEL interventions show these positive life outcomes, which impact students far into adulthood. Students can reap the benefits of having had a HEART-filled educator even when they are adults! That's a legacy worth pursuing, don't you think?

Effective teachers cultivate positive relationships with students not only at the beginning of the school year but every day, in the physical *and* the virtual classroom. They foster emotional connections with and among students, and they create an environment where students feel physically and emotionally safe and have a sense of belonging and purpose. This is not a small task; in fact, it is possibly one of the most important things an educator can do to create conditions that will support students as they grow academically, socially, and emotionally. The good news is that, as an educator, you can design and implement practices that support this growth. In this chapter, we will learn more about the importance of relationships and how we can apply these findings in the classroom.

RELATIONSHIPS INFLUENCE HUMAN DEVELOPMENT

Human development is not predetermined, fixed, or linear; it is unique to each individual and highly responsive to environments, cultures, and relationships. This means that individuals and contexts mutually influence and shape each other. Our brains are continually adapting, (re)organizing, and changing in response to what we experience and how we make sense of these experiences.

According to the latest research in developmental science, relationships between and among children and adults are "a primary process through which biological and contextual factors influence and mutually reinforce each other." [29] Positive relationships not only create the developmental pathways for lifelong learning, adaptation, and integration of social, emotional, and cognitive skills but also make qualitative changes to a child's genetic makeup. Our brains are *malleable,* and they change in response to the experiences, relationships, and environments we encounter from birth into adulthood.

At the same time, enriching contexts provide children with assets that foster their resilience, therefore reducing their vulnerability and the impact that negative factors may have on their development. Enriching contexts serve to develop protective factors in children. Researchers from the Center on the Developing Child at Harvard University explain that these positive experiences, support from adults, and the development of adaptive skills can counterbalance the lifelong consequences of adversity.[30] Furthermore, these researchers found that children who have overcome hardships *almost always* have had at least one stable and responsive relationship with a parent, caregiver, or other adult who provided vital support and helped them build effective coping skills.

Although the brain has the capacity to learn from experience, its receptivity for learning is greatest early in life and decreases with age. For this reason, it is harder (although still possible) to change behavior or build new skills when brain circuits have not been wired from the beginning.

Providing these enriched environments with the ingredients for healthy development will support students as they overcome the effects of adversity and increase the likelihood of better outcomes.

The unprecedented challenges to student well-being caused by COVID-19 have made clear the need to deeply invest in SEL, with a focus on improving student mental health and social connectedness. Research on health-related crises and disasters shows that 30 percent of isolated or quarantined children experienced post-traumatic stress disorder.[31] Fostering strong relationships and supporting children to build HEART skills can promote wellness and "mitigate negative effects of trauma in both the short and long term."[32] In a world fighting to respond to the challenges of a global pandemic, the need for connection and bonding with our students becomes even greater.

As teachers struggle to do what they can to fight the many challenges and injustices that children and youth often face (lack of access to resources, health care, healthy food), they can shape children's growth in constructive ways through the power of relationships. Teachers can make a positive impact in a child's life by nurturing an emotional connection and a trusting relationship. If you had a student who was going through a time without an engaged adult relationship available, could you be that stable and responsive relationship that could make a major difference in their life?

WHAT ARE THE CHARACTERISTICS OF POSITIVE RELATIONSHIPS?

As an educator, you may dream of starting the school year with a positive and supportive classroom environment already established. Wouldn't that be nice? The reality is, however, that supportive environments conducive to learning and healthy development don't just appear; teachers build them over time through consistent and important teaching practices. The same is true for developing a positive relationship with students. It requires that we pay attention to our own HEART skills, using them to build trust that ensures the physical and emotional safety of our students, enabling them to belong and to have a sense of purpose in our classroom.

The latest studies that investigate teacher-student relationships[33] identify several elements that influence this relationship. The following list is not comprehensive, but it summarizes the core aspects that educators can develop and incorporate into their practice, nurturing positive relationships with students.

EMOTIONAL CONNECTION

This refers to our capacity to connect with our students and establish a bond. We show our emotional connection through our facial expressions, body language, and tone of voice. The way we listen to our students—not only the words they say but also the meaning of what they say—is an expression of this connection as well. Establishing this emotional connection starts with educators connecting with students and sharing their own feelings; when students see their teachers share their emotions, they will be more inclined to share their own.

Bonding with students does not mean that we carry home their challenges, but that we are able to relate to their feelings and what they bring to the classroom. This is one of the most challenging aspects of the teaching profession; too often educators feel overwhelmed by the injustices that their students experience and the desire to fix them. To maintain a balance, it is important that you establish healthy boundaries that will allow you to be responsive to your students while also giving yourself space to take care of your own needs.

Strategies for Establishing Emotional Connections

- **Create opportunities to talk with students about non-school things.** Students love sharing thoughts about their favorite sports team, TV show, or food. Make a habit of talking with your students about things they like to do outside of school. If you have a hard time remembering who likes what, have students make a list of their favorite things, then regularly ask about them.

- **Let students get to know you as a person.** Share some things about yourself with your students: your hobbies, what you like to do during the weekend, or your favorite activities as a child. When appropriate, also share stories about times when you overcame a difficult situation or made a mistake. Opening up with students indicates that it is safe for them to do the same.

- **Communicate a belief in your students' capacity to learn and act on it.** Effective teachers expect great things from their students, genuinely believe that their students are brilliant and capable, and provide appropriate levels of autonomy and support for each child. Providing an appropriate level of support to meet students' needs communicates a belief in their capacity to learn and grow. Given the biases that we have acquired from living in a society that discriminates against BIPOC, educators may need to examine these harmful beliefs and work to counter them. Only when students know that their teacher honestly believes in them, can a respectful relationship between learner and educator be established.

TRUSTWORTHINESS

In my experience, trust is at the heart of any successful relationship. It allows for honest communication, a sense of respect toward the other person, and maybe even a shared purpose. Creating a classroom where teachers trust students and students trust teachers has many benefits: students are more likely to improve their academic performance, more willing to follow class rules, and more likely to engage with the content and ask questions. In addition, there are several studies that show that when teachers trust their students, their pedagogy changes; they share more classroom control with students,[34] for instance, or are more likely to engage in constructivist practices or differentiated instruction.[35]

Teachers' trust in students also plays a crucial role in students' social integration and sense of belonging in school. But what is trust? And how can we give and earn it?

Trust is something that you feel; it is an emotion, a basic human signal that helps us survive and thrive. When we don't trust a person, our emotions are signaling, "this is not okay," which might cause us to disengage, ignore the person, or fight back. Try to remember a boss or a colleague that you didn't trust. Were you able to fully express yourself? Did you feel safe in the relationship? Did this person trust you? The answer to each of these questions is probably "no." Trust is reciprocal and also contagious. If you don't trust your students, you'll rarely gain trust *from* them. The same is true the other way around; if a student doesn't trust you, you will probably have a hard time trusting them.

Differences in social and cultural backgrounds and circumstances make it harder to trust others. For instance, BIPOC students and their families may have a hard time trusting their White teachers, given the existing institutionalized racism in US schools. At the same time, White teachers may not be inclined to trust their BIPOC students due to their own bias and learned beliefs. This trust gap may hinder academic success for minorities—middle school students who lose trust in their teachers are less likely to attend college even if they generally had good grades, according to psychology research from the University of Texas at Austin.[36] Without seeing these patterns, teachers will not be able to do the work to counter them and build authentic trust. We must recognize this challenge, and put in the work to break this cycle.

Strategies to Earn Your Students' Trust

- **Be honest.** The way you show up for class affects your students' emotions and their dispositions to learn. If you are upset or stressed, your students will be too; emotions are contagious. Being honest also means avoiding gaps between what you say and what your students perceive. Check for understanding, and when you commit to doing something with or for your students, follow through.

- **Be coherent.** Model the behavior you hope your students will display in class. Check your goals, classroom routines, and assignments; are they aligned? If you want students to show initiative, create opportunities for them to make choices about how they learn. If you encourage students to provide feedback, do something with it! Being coherent means that you are consistent (in your expectations and classroom structures) as well as reliable (you do what you say you'll do).

- **See the humanity in all your students.** You can foster genuine connections when you *show* students that you care. The emphasis here is not the caring (which I know you do), but the showing. Have you recently had a non-school-related chat with students who display challenging behaviors? Those informal conversations can go a long way in furthering your efforts to give and earn your students' trust. Celebrate students' accomplishments (big and small), and persevere in getting to know them. Show that you care for them without conditions; every student knows you care just by being in your classroom.

- **Trust yourself.** Trust starts with you. In order to trust your students, you need to trust yourself first. Even when you make mistakes or things don't go as you had planned, show yourself some compassion. Have faith in yourself.

CULTURAL RESPONSIVENESS

Understanding students' lives can help educators foster positive relationships and ensure that students feel respected and seen in the classroom. Culture is central to student learning; cultural practices shape students' thinking processes, which serve as tools for learning in and outside of school.[37] Educators who are culturally responsive to their students respect their languages, cultures, and life experiences as meaningful sources for learning and understanding.

Teachers can learn about the cultures represented in their classroom and translate this knowledge to create a safe learning environment by first developing a bicultural lens. This means that educators (almost 80 percent of whom were White in the 2017-18 school year, according to the National Center for Education Statistics[38]) get out of their own community and visit the neighborhoods where their students live—go to their grocery stores and eat at their favorite restaurants. What's the environment like? Then, watch some of their favorite movies and read the magazines that they love. As Zaretta Hammond, author of *Culturally Responsive Teaching and the Brain*, says, "You need to put yourself in a place where you are not the majority."[39]

Secondly, educators need to build their racial literacy, so they can understand how the sociopolitical context negatively impacts BIPOC students— inequitable systems of school finance, small numbers of qualified teachers choosing to work in schools with a majority of BIPOC students, and being consistently sent to lower-track classes regardless of skill level, among other inequities—make a tremendous difference to children's learning. Becoming racially literate also means that teachers learn and teach about the contributions, assets, and richness of BIPOC cultures, not only their struggles.

At the same time, students experience microaggressions in and outside of school on a regular basis. These are insults, indignities, and denigrating messages that come out in everyday interpersonal situations and show the implicit bias students and adults carry. For example, being told, "Go back to Mexico" or, "Oh, you're so articulate" or being asked "How did *you* get into that program/school?" are a few comments that occur all the time.

When students have to face hostile environments, they use most of their cognitive and emotional skills for dealing with the challenges rather than for learning. On the other hand, when safe and supportive environments are created, and students' unique traits and life experiences are acknowledged, celebrated, and used to enrich the learning environment, students are more likely to feel a sense of belonging and engage with the classroom content in meaningful ways.

In order for this to be possible, teachers need to develop their *cultural competence*, that is to develop an awareness of one's own cultural identity (What is my cultural group reference? How does my prior experience influence my teaching?) and views about differences. It also means developing an ability to learn about and build on the varying cultural and community assets of students and their families that connect academic instruction with students' prior knowledge and experiences. Educators also need to understand the negative impact that implicit bias and microaggressions have on students' academic, social, and emotional growth and make sure to promote an inclusive and equitable classroom that proactively works to counteract and reverse implicit bias.

In the US, the elementary and secondary teacher workforce is not as racially diverse as the population at-large or the student body. While almost 80 percent of teachers in public schools are White, approximately half (49 percent) of public elementary and secondary school students are people of color. This is a significant diversity gap; students of color need positive role models, who look like them, in schools. Teachers who share their students' backgrounds have the potential to make a profound impact on their students. A 2018 report from the Learning Policy Institute, "Diversifying the Teaching Profession: How to Recruit and Retain Teachers of Color," found that teachers of color boost the academic performance of students of color.[40] Both students of color and White students report having positive perceptions of their teachers of color, including feeling cared for and academically challenged.

Having a diverse classroom is exciting. It will challenge you to create a space where students can bring the pride they feel for their race and ethnicity, and develop an appreciation for diverse racial and ethnic identities. If your students are mostly White, you can *intentionally* equip them with tools to fight injustice, and face racism with a sense of collective responsibility and humility. For starters, one of the most effective tools you can use is your ability to get to know your students and develop positive relationships with them.

Strategies for Developing Cultural Competence

- **Learn about yourself.** If there is one thing that I would like you to take away from this book it is that self-knowledge is the basis for SEL. If you are able to identify your historical roots, your beliefs and values, the way culture has influenced your life, the things that motivate and matter to you, and your implicit bias, then you will more likely be able to support others in developing their skills.

- **Learn about each of your students.** What is their ethnic group? What is their home language and religion? Are any of your students newly arrived immigrants or refugees? Even if students identify with a single ethnic group, don't make assumptions about their values or beliefs. Get to know your students individually, while also learning about the history and culture of their identities.

- **Get to know your students' families.** Parents also experience emotions about their children's school and teachers; they may fear their child is being mistreated or bullied, they may distrust a teacher whose culture is not the same as theirs, or they may question a teacher's suitability because the classroom doesn't look like the classroom they attended when they were kids. Whatever their feelings toward you or the school, remember that their emotions are real. Of course, you may not agree with them, but that's a different story.

- **Begin by meeting your students' parents.** This can take the shape of a family potluck, a getting-to-know-you back-to-school night, home visits, or phone calls to celebrate students' accomplishments. The goal of these interactions is for you to develop important connections with the families: to learn about their beliefs, hopes, and dreams and to learn how they perceive your role in supporting their children's education.

  Elena Aguilar, founder of Bright Morning Consulting and author of *The Art of Coaching*, encourages teachers to let families know that they want to learn about their individual cultures, acknowledging the differences that exist. Many immigrant parents worry that their home culture will be forgotten when kids go to school. For parents, it can be a big relief knowing that their child's teacher wants to learn about their culture. Inviting parents into the classroom is also a great way to celebrate and share students' cultures.

- **Learn about the community.** This is an extension of knowing your students and their families. Walking around a neighborhood and understanding the community's assets—the food, music, traditions, or history of the neighborhood—as well as some of the issues they face can provide you with important data to connect with your students and to inform your teaching. How does the community celebrate special holidays? How has the neighborhood changed in the last decade? Are some of the parents facing unemployment or housing challenges? How is that affecting the student population that the school serves? Approach this process with curiosity and without judgment; what can you learn that can help you better serve your students? And what can you learn from your immediate reactions to the neighborhood that can help you to examine and counter your own biases?

TAKEAWAYS AND NEXT STEPS

Human relationships are among the essential ingredients for learning and human development. Positive, consistent experiences support optimal brain development and have an important protective effect on children and adolescents. Students who report having a positive relationship with their teachers have better academic results and a greater sense of belonging. As an educator, you can develop positive, caring relationships with your students by cultivating an emotional connection, a sense of trust, and by counteracting your own bias and affirming your students' identity.

Now, find a pencil and a piece of paper and answer the following questions:

	Main Ideas What are the key takeaways for you from this chapter?
	Insights What did you think while you were reading? How did you feel? What surprised you?
	Direction What does this mean for your work as an educator? What one or two actions will you be taking to develop relationships with your students?

Endnotes

27 Darling-Hammond, Linda, and Channa M. Cook-Harvey. "Educating the Whole Child: Improving School Climate to Support Student Success." Learning Policy Institute. September 2018.

28 Williford, Amanda P., and Catherine Sanger Wolcott. "SEL and Student-Teacher Relationships." In *Handbook of Social Emotional Learning: Research and Practice* edited by Joseph A. Durlak, Celine E. Domitrovich, Roger P. Weissberg, and Thomas P. Gullotta. New York, NY: Guilford Press, 2016.

29 Osher, David, Pamela Cantor, Juliette Berg, Lily Steyer, and Todd Rose. "Drivers of Human Development: How relationships and context shape learning and development." *Applied Developmental Science* 24, no. 2 (January 2018): 1-31. https://doi.org/10.1080/10888691.201 7.1398650.

30 "From Best Practices to Breakthrough Impacts: A Science-Based Approach to Building a More Promising Future for Young Children and Families." Center on the Developing Child at Harvard University. 2016. https://developingchild.harvard.edu/resources/from-best-practices-to-breakthrough-impacts/.

31 Sprang, Ginny, and Miriam Silman. "Posttraumatic stress disorder in parents and youth after health-related disasters." *Disaster Medicine and Public Health Preparedness* 7, no. 1 (February 2013): 105–10. https://doi.org/10.1017/dmp.2013.22.

32 Cipriano, Christina, Gabrielle Rappolt-Schlichtmann, and Marc Brackett. "Supporting School Community Wellness with Social and Emotional Learning (SEL) During and After a Pandemic." PennState College of Health and Human Development. August 2020. https://www.prevention.psu.edu/uploads/files/PSU-SEL-Crisis-Brief.pdf.

33 Osher, "Drivers of Human Development," 1-31.

34 Goddard, Roger, Megan Tschannen-Moran, and Wayne K. Hoy. "A Multilevel Examination of the Distribution and Effects of Teacher Trust in Students and Parents in Urban Elementary Schools." *The Elementary School Journal* 102, no. 1 (September 2001): 3-17. https://doi.org/10.1086/499690.

35 Rainer, Julie, Edi Guyton, and Christie Bowen. "Constructivist Pedagogy in Primary Classrooms." Paper presented at the Annual Conference of the American Educational Research Association. New Orleans. April 24–28, 2000.

36 Yeager, David, Valerie Purdie-Vaughns, Sophia Yang Hooper, and Geoffrey L. Cohen. "Loss of Institutional Trust Among Racial and Ethnic Minority Adolescents: A Consequence of Procedural Injustice and a Cause of Life-Span Outcomes." *Child Development* 88, no. 2 (February 2017): 658–676. https://doi.org/10.1111/cdev.12697.

37 Hammond, Zaretta. *Culturally Responsive Teaching and the Brain: Promoting Authentic Engagement and Rigor Among Culturally and Linguistically Diverse Students*. Thousand Oaks, CA: Corwin, 2014.

38 "Race and Ethnicity of Public Schools Teachers and Their Students." National Center for Education Statistics, September 2020. https://nces.ed.gov/pubs2020/2020103.pdf

39 Hammond, Zaretta. "You Could Be 'Woker' than You Think." Facebook. July 30, 2020.

40 Carver-Thomas, Desiree. "Diversifying the Teaching Profession: How to Recruit and Retain Teachers of Color." Learning Policy Institute. April 19, 2020. https://learningpolicyinstitute.org/product/diversifying-teaching-profession-report.

Chapter 3: Adversity Affects Learning

David was a fifth grader at an elementary school in East Oakland, California, where I worked as a special education teacher. The school was in a neighborhood greatly affected by crime, drugs, and gangs. Several students at the school had been exposed to violence and abuse, and most of the students had experienced some kind of psychological trauma.

David loved drawing comics and often played basketball during recess. He liked math, especially solving problems with manipulatives. He was reading at a second-grade level, and although he was not the only one in the classroom who was behind in reading, he felt ashamed. I saw David twice a week to work on his reading. The minute he walked into my room, I could clearly see whether he was doing well or having a hard day. When he felt defeated, frustrated, or pushed in any way, he would shut down and not respond to any verbal communication. The other teachers who worked with him and I would often discuss what else we could do to support him. David had only been at the school for one year, and he would leave at the end of fifth grade. We didn't have a lot of time with him.

I met with his mother on several occasions to discuss David's progress. She was unemployed and dealing with drug addiction. I always wondered what it was like for David to go home after school. Did he have a safe place to sleep? Did he eat a warm meal? Did he receive words of encouragement? It was difficult to watch how much pain he carried and realize that we weren't doing enough to *really* help him. After David finished fifth grade, I lost track of him. I still remember how helpless I felt the day we said goodbye.

In the US, 34.8 million children are affected by Adverse Childhood Experiences (ACEs), which are stressful or traumatic events that children experience before age 18, such as poverty, violence at home, neglect, abuse, or having a parent with mental illness or substance dependence.[41] ACEs harm children's developing brains, leading to changes in how they respond to stress and damaging their immune systems with effects that manifest well into adulthood. In the first large-scale epidemiological study conducted by the US Centers for Disease Control and Prevention and Kaiser Permanente in 1998, researchers repeatedly found a *graded and dose-response relationship* between ACEs and negative health and well-being outcomes across a life course.[42] That is to say, as the number of stressors increased for an individual, so did the intensity of developing risk factors for disease throughout the life course.

This study was conducted in a population that was 70 percent Caucasian and 70 percent college-educated. As patients of Kaiser, the study's participants also had great health care. The dominant view that poverty and lack of adequate health care drove poor health outcomes started to shake after this ACE study was published. Further studies have validated these findings—adverse childhood experiences in and of themselves are a risk factor for many of the most common and serious diseases in the United States and across the globe, regardless of income, race, or access to care.

According to the Centers for Disease Control and Prevention, children who have experienced ACEs have a higher risk for:

- Alcoholism and alcohol abuse
- Chronic obstructive pulmonary disease
- Multiple sexual partners
- Sexually transmitted diseases

- Depression
- Fetal death
- Health-related quality of life
- Illicit drug use
- Ischemic heart disease
- Liver disease
- Poor work performance
- Financial stress
- Risk for intimate partner violence

- Smoking
- Suicide attempts
- Unintended pregnancies
- Early initiation of smoking
- Early initiation of sexual activity
- Adolescent pregnancy
- Risk for sexual violence
- Poor academic achievement

A high or frequent exposure to ACEs disrupts a child's developing brain, affecting their social, emotional, and cognitive growth. When the toxic stress that students experience is not treated, they may have health concerns and develop mental health issues such as depression, anxiety, substance abuse, or suicide. Many children exposed to severe or frequent ACEs also develop learning disabilities and, as students, may have difficulties with attention, concentration, memory, and creativity. These students may be perceived by teachers and caregivers as unwilling to follow directions, defiant, or disengaged when, in fact, there are significant causes affecting their ability to develop a healthy stress response system. Early screening for adversity can help pediatricians and educators identify and treat children at risk of a lifetime of health issues.

When students have been exposed to toxic stress, their stress hormones overwhelm their bodies and brains. Everyday situations, such as a loud noise from a book falling onto the floor or a change in the daily schedule, can trigger a fight-or-flight response. These students tend to have fewer tools to cope with normal, everyday stressful situations, like taking a test in school, in part because their brains and bodies may react as if these small challenges were real threats to their survival. Toxic stress impacts individuals' ability to use their HEART skills.

Types of Stress

Positive Stress	Tolerable Stress	Toxic Stress
The body responds to normal, everyday stress, like getting to school on time or taking a test.	The body responds to more serious stress, like living through a natural disaster or a scary injury.	The body responds to severe and/or lasting stress, such as emotional or physical abuse or neglect.
Stress hormones help the body do what is needed in the moment, but once the event passes, our body goes back to its normal state.	A flood of stress hormones helps the body rise to the occasion, putting us on alert. However, the presence of a caring and trusted adult can offset this rush, calming the child's stress response and building resilience.	The stress hormones overwhelm the child's body and brain. Without the support from a caring and trusted adult, it can result in lifelong issues with mental and physical health as well as behavior.

Source: Adapted from the Center for Youth Wellness

At the same time, exposure to toxic stress affects children's sense of security. If the parent-child relationship has been inconsistent, interrupted, or unhealthy, it will be difficult for kids to know if they can trust other adults. For example, when a teacher says, "Put away these books, and then you can go to recess," a child might not believe that the second action is really going to happen and may decide that it's not worth putting away the books. Insecure attachment patterns established with the early caregivers will be projected onto future relationships, and it will take repeated and consistent positive experiences with adults for these children to create new relationship patterns.

Dr. Tish Jennings, an internationally recognized leader in the fields of social and emotional learning and mindfulness in education, explains that teachers *can* create a new template for children's assessment of adults; students can learn that teachers are caring and kind people who want to help them.[43] This is especially important for early childhood educators and lower school teachers. The sooner a child can see teachers as caring and helpful adults, the sooner this kid will be able to enjoy the benefits of going to school.

The degree to which ACEs impact a student's growth and development, and the stress levels associated with these experiences, may differ depending on the particular child and/or the situation. For example, while a home where parents are going through a divorce can create a lot of stress, in some cases leaving an abusive parent to live with a stable one may actually reduce the amount of stress in a child's life. In addition, students who have had the same exposure to ACEs may cope with stress in differing ways, depending on whether they received effective interventions from doctors and educators, and were able to reduce or eliminate the exposure to toxic stress.

You may feel helpless in the face of this research, knowing the many challenges that children and youth experience. However, children and youth *can* have experiences that protect and help them develop resilience despite exposure to ACEs. As an educator, you are a protective factor for these students. You can become a different template for a child who has been exposed to toxic stress and who doesn't trust other adults. In this next section, we will discuss what you can do in your classroom to develop students' resilience.

SUPPORTING STUDENTS TO BUILD RESILIENCE

A few years back I volunteered at a local high school, supporting senior students with their college applications. Most of them were the first in their families to apply for college. One year, my mentee was Carolina. A confident, driven, and hard-working student, Carolina was on track to graduate with honors despite the difficult circumstances she had faced growing up. She came to the United States illegally with her mother and three siblings when she was six years old, escaping a violent father. Carolina's mom worked different jobs to provide for the family, and they had to move several times, fearing deportation. The mother had told Carolina to focus on one thing and one thing only: her education. However, Carolina often had to care for her siblings, make dinner, and pack lunches before her mom got home from work.

When I met Carolina, she knew exactly what she wanted to study in college: education. She wanted to become a teacher and help other kids who were going through similar circumstances. She loved school and felt an obligation to give back to the community.

Carolina enrolled in a state university and got a part-time job. After two years, she transferred to a community college because she couldn't afford the university tuition and she wanted to be closer to her mom. She now works in customer service at a software company and is two classes away from finishing her bachelor's degree.

Carolina was exposed to adverse childhood experiences: witnessing violence against her mother, the stress of moving numerous times, the fear of being deported. Despite these circumstances, Carolina persevered. She was a model student in high school and wants to finish her college degree. A combination of her personal characteristics, her mother's support, and caring teachers who believed in her helped Carolina lessen the negative impact of her childhood experiences.

Research shows that the right kind of support and care can mitigate the impact of toxic stress in children and help them bounce back.[44] Individuals, families, and communities can influence the development of many protective factors throughout a child's life. Effective treatment of ACEs requires a *coordinated community effort* that can effectively provide support for children, youth, and families. This is not something you can do alone. However, there are things you can do in the classroom to better support students who have experienced trauma.

TRAUMA-INFORMED PRACTICES

You may be wondering how many students in your classroom have had or are currently experiencing trauma and toxic stress. In certain cases, you may receive information from the school's counselor or psychologist or, if the student has one, from their Individualized Educational Plan (IEP). However, in many cases students don't share what is happening; they may fear harsh punishment from their caregiver or being told they are lying. In other cases, they may not be able to put their experience into words. Therefore, there might be students in your classroom who have ACEs that you don't know about. The good news is that trauma-informed practices benefit *all* students, so you don't need to know for sure if students are experiencing toxic stress to embrace these strategies.

When I was studying to become a special education teacher, there was a big push to generalize the use of effective strategies to support learning differences in the general education classroom. Until that point, teachers used certain tools with special education students only, believing that the other students did not need them. Well, teachers started to realize that many of these strategies benefited not only students who had been diagnosed with a disability but other students as well. The same is true for trauma-informed practices; they don't need to be reserved for those students who you know for certain have been exposed to adversity. Trauma-informed practices will support *all* students in your classroom.

Nurture supportive relationships. If you skipped Chapter Two, this would be a good time to go back and read it. If you read it, you know that positive student-teacher relationships are essential for healthy development and they set up the foundation for life-long learning. Dr. Tish Jennings emphasizes that for students who experience trauma, a supportive and warm classroom environment is a *necessity*.[45] Therefore, get to know your students and focus on their strengths, even when students are exhibiting difficulties. If you make a point to identify students' strengths, you will be able to connect with them despite some of their challenging behaviors.

When you offer an unconditional positive regard for each student—one that is not contingent on compliance, finishing work, or good grades—students learn that *they* are worthy of care, just for being who they are. This is a powerful lesson for students and one that is not so easy for teachers to execute. It truly requires that educators use HEART skills such as empathy and compassion to see the child behind the behavior and to say to the child, "Tell me what happened and how you felt, I am here for you."

Create physically and emotionally safe spaces. David, my former student, would sometimes come to my room when he was not doing well. He would look around as if trying to find something to do; sometimes he sat down, even if I was working with other students. His teacher and I had agreed that David could come to my room if he was feeling overwhelmed in his busy fifth-grade classroom. He generally wanted to read comic books, which he did for a few minutes before returning to his classroom. Although his teacher and I knew that this arrangement interrupted his class work, we also knew that unless he felt cared for and had a safe space to manage his emotions, he would not be able to focus on learning.

For learning to take place, a child needs to feel safe, physically and emotionally. While most classrooms are physically safe, many could use a more emotionally healthy environment. When students feel shamed, intimidated, or scared on a regular basis, they become disengaged and less motivated about school. This disengagement may contribute to poor attendance, grade repetition, and discipline referrals, which, in turn, may lead to school dropout.[46] In other words, when schools do not foster the appropriate conditions for learning, including positive relationships between and among students and adults, schools can actually harm students.

As we saw in Chapter One, it is fine to experience a wide range of different emotions in school; however, learning environments cannot be built on frustration or fear, because they cause the brain to go into a flight-or-fight response. For a child who has experienced trauma and adversity, it is important to encounter an environment of respect and care, establishing healthy boundaries and expectations that are shared by students and teachers.

The existence of exclusionary policies, such as suspensions and expulsions, severely affect students who experience toxic stress—they cause feelings of rejection and low self-worth. These measures also break the ties between the student and the school, leading to a lack of trust toward teachers and the school as an institution.

For these reasons, it is recommended that students participate in the process of creating behavior expectations for the classroom—expectations that consider students' needs. This helps students who have experienced ACEs take the driver's seat in their own learning and development. When expectations are created as a collaborative task, students tend to be more invested not only in following them but also in helping others get on board with the agreed plan.

While many teachers may feel the need to create ideal conditions so students do not have outbursts (i.e., by avoiding the things that trigger students), the reality is that educators cannot control everything that happens inside or outside the classroom. However, they can decrease the number and intensity of these outbursts by teaching students healthy ways to understand and manage their emotions, so they can make better choices. These self-management skills will support students' success not only in the classroom but also when working with other students and in other environments.

We should not lower our expectations for students' academic, social, and emotional growth. On the contrary, we should maintain expectations while providing the supports needed for these students with specific needs to get to where they need to be. Students who have had adverse experiences as children *can* grow up to be healthy, contributing adults, given the appropriate support. A powerful example is the story of Vinny Ferraro.[47]

Ferraro is a long-time mindfulness practitioner and trainer for Mindful Schools. Listening to his soft and compassionate guided meditations, you would never imagine that he sold drugs in New Haven, Connecticut, when he was only 15 years old and smuggled heroin into jail for his incarcerated dad. At the age of 20, he was addicted to crack and weighed 110 pounds. After recovering from drug addiction, he started to speak to heroin addicts at rehabilitation centers and juvenile halls. Finally, he had found something that he was good at besides fighting and selling drugs. Since that time, Ferraro has led workshops for over 110,000 youth as the director of training for Challenge Day, a nationally recognized school-based emotional intelligence and life-skills program. He is a teacher and director with the Mind Body Awareness Project, a mindfulness-based curriculum for incarcerated youth, and he teaches at mindfulness retreats for adults in the US and around the world.

Ferraro's story exemplifies how adverse childhood experiences can greatly influence, but not determine, who you become as an adult and how you decide to use these early negative experiences. In Ferraro's case, he chose to use them as a way to connect with youth living in similar circumstances to his own and supporting their fight for a different future. He also embraced mindfulness and has been practicing meditation since the early nineties. Ferraro says his desire is to make a difference by sharing his story and using a mindfulness and social-emotional learning approach. In Ferraro's words from a 2018 interview:[48]

"The practice helps me in so many ways. I felt alone in the world, and now I feel like in some ways I belong to the world and that my gift to this world is my heart. So when they hear about my history, that puts them at ease. And there's a transmission that happens, and they feel like 'if this dude could do it, maybe I could do it.'"

Too many children carry a heavy weight of stress and trauma, which can follow them into adulthood, impacting their ability to live a healthy and fulfilling life. However, a HEART-filled classroom with a caring and supportive teacher can truly make a difference in a child's life. By creating a physically and emotionally safe place for students, you are planting the seeds for changing the odds for students like David and for Vinny Ferraro.

Teach and support self-management skills. As we have seen, ACEs can drastically change a child's developing brain, often interfering with a healthy social and emotional development. This means that, in certain cases, students with ACEs will not use the same coping and self-soothing strategies you would expect other students to use at the same age. They often struggle with emotion regulation, which makes it hard for them to work in groups or to persevere to solve problems and finish school work. Educators working with students exposed to trauma can support students' growth and readiness for learning in two ways:

1. By explicitly teaching emotional literacy to help students name their emotions and by teaching mindfulness practices, such as using the breath to calm down. We will go into detail about the HEART skills of self-awareness (Honoring Your Emotions) and self-management (Electing Your Responses) in Chapter Five.

2. By supporting students when you notice they are getting agitated or frustrated. You can help students calm down, for example, by using a soothing, comforting voice or by offering them the use of a calming corner *before* the outburst happens.

Although you will not always be able to anticipate changes in a schedule or the likelihood of certain activities becoming chaotic, you can be a steady, consistent, and trustworthy figure for these students. They will need additional opportunities to learn and practice self-management skills, which you can structure following a tiered intervention, just as you would with your academic instruction.

Take care of yourself. Some teachers may find it difficult to connect with students whose behaviors are challenging to manage in the classroom. It may become hard to "see" the student and the story behind the disruptive behavior. In other cases, teachers are so aware of students' traumatic experiences that they become overprotective or too involved with the student. In either case the consequences are similar: trauma in students' lives takes an emotional and physical toll on teachers as well. Turnover among teachers is high at schools in low socioeconomic-status neighborhoods due to the burnout that results from working with students living in poverty and exposed to trauma in their lives.[49] This turnover puts students at an increased disadvantage because the teacher-student relationship has been broken, and many vacated positions are filled with unqualified teachers.

It is important for teachers to take care of themselves, and schools should plan accordingly. I have witnessed how teachers become restless and disengaged when staff meetings leave no space for them to connect with one another and transition from the classroom to the staff room. I have also experienced how a few minutes of mindfulness or gratitude at the beginning of a meeting helps teachers to get grounded and present, ready to engage with others. No matter what type of school you teach in, you can do things to take care of yourself, thus ensuring that you will be able to find purpose and joy in working with your students. Your well-being is *almost* a prerequisite to develop your students' resilience. In section three of this book, we go deeper into becoming a whole-hearted educator.

According to the Center for Youth Wellness, there are several elements that can support students in developing a healthy stress response:[50]

- Supportive relationships
- Balanced nutrition
- Regular exercise/physical activity
- Quality sleep
- Mental health care
- Mindfulness practices

TAKEAWAYS AND NEXT STEPS

Teachers have a key role in supporting students who have been exposed to trauma and adversity. These students can have experiences that protect and help them develop resilience despite exposure to ACEs. As an educator, you can become a protective factor for these students by nurturing a positive relationship, creating a safe space in the classroom, and teaching HEART skills. Using self-care strategies will support your energy and commitment to this work.

Now, find a pencil and a piece of paper and answer the following questions:

	Main Ideas What are the key takeaways for you from this chapter?
	Insights What did you think while you were reading? How did you feel? What surprised you?
	Direction What does this mean for your work as an educator? What one or two actions will you be taking to implement trauma-informed practices in your classroom?

Endnotes

41   "Adversity and toxic stress are so pervasive, they affect us all." Center for Youth Wellness. Accessed September 23, 2020, from https://centerforyouthwellness.org/ace-toxic-stress/.

42   Felitti, V. J., R. F. Anda, D. Nordenberg, D. F. Williamson, A. M. Spitz, V. Edwards, and J. S. Marks. "Relationship of childhood abuse and household dysfunction to many of the leading causes of death in adults: The Adverse Childhood Experiences (ACE) Study." *American Journal of Preventive Medicine* 14, no. 4 (May 1998): 245-258. https://doi.org/10.1016/s0749-3797(98)00017-8.

43   Jennings, Patricia. *The Trauma-Sensitive Classroom: Building Resilience with Compassionate Teaching.* New York: W. W. Norton & Company, 2018.

44   "Young Children Develop in an Environment of Relationships: Working Paper No. 1." National Scientific Council on the Developing Child. Updated October 2009. https://46y5e-h11fhgw3ve3ytpwxt9r-wpengine.netdna-ssl.com/wp-content/uploads/2004/04/Young-Children-Develop-in-an-Environment-of-Relationships.pdf.

45   Jennings, *The Trauma-Sensitive Classroom.*

46   Osher, David, Pamela Cantor, Juliette Berg, Lily Steyer, and Todd Rose. "Drivers of Human Development: How relationships and context shape learning and development." *Applied Developmental Science* 24, no. 2 (January 2018): 1-31. https://doi.org/10.1080/10888691.2017.1398650.

47   Sharkey, Alix. "The Heartful Dodger." *Tricycle.* Spring 2010. https://thejusticeartscoalition.org/wp-content/uploads/2011/07/the-heartful-dodger.pdf.

48   Wilson, Tamara. "He lived in a crack house. Now he's guiding people out of addiction, with meditation." *CNN.* Updated August 31, 2018. https://www.cnn.com/2018/08/31/health/turning-points-vinny-ferraro/index.html.

49   Izard, Ernest. "Teaching Children from Poverty and Trauma." National Education Association. https://files.eric.ed.gov/fulltext/ED594465.pdf.

50   "Childhood adversity increases risk for long-term health and behavioral issues." Center for Youth Wellness. Accessed September 23, 2020, https://centerforyouthwellness.org/health-impacts/.

PART 2: TEACHING AND LEARNING WITH THE HEART IN MIND

Chapter 4: Developing Positive Conditions for Learning

I believe that SEL can become a tool for social progress when we use the HEART in Mind model *in service of* equity and social justice. That means:

- Justice is not an afterthought or an add-on to our curriculum but a way of being and relating to ourselves and others in the classroom.

- Relationship-centered learning environments are cultivated to support individuals in becoming the best versions of themselves, which includes having difficult conversations about systemic and structural racism, discrimination, privilege, and other complex topics.

- Intellectually safe environments are created where students are asked to do high-level problem solving and are expected to engage in higher-order thinking tasks.[51]

Writer and former elementary school teacher Bret Turner warns of "focusing on the dream of an equitable future without teaching the reality of an inequitable present."[52] We are doing our students a disservice if we don't confront the many limiting beliefs in our society; in many cases, they are based on stereotypes, unconscious bias, or plain ignorance. We cannot ignore them, because they deeply influence the ways in which we behave and relate to others, sometimes reinforcing these stereotypes and contributing to inequitable practices. We start by analyzing how our own limiting beliefs may influence our teaching and the expectations we hold about our students, so we can become more effective educators and support students in doing high cognitive work. Then, we proceed to help others in doing the same.

This can be our most important contribution to closing the opportunity gap for students who have been underserved by the current educational system—give them the academic, social, and emotional tools they need to be successful in a 21st century world where technologies, access to information, and work processes are rapidly changing. Students will need to develop skills such as critical thinking, problem solving, applying their knowledge in different situations, and the ability to self-direct, in order to complete important projects and activities. They will also need empathy and compassion to connect with others, and cultural competence to navigate a complex and diverse world.

When educators teach with the HEART in mind, they can create the *social and emotional conditions* in the classroom that will support deeper learning; there needs to be trust among the members of the group, physical and emotional safety, and a sense of belonging, purpose, and connection. Teachers must build this atmosphere over time by consistently implementing the crucial practices presented in this book and inviting students to engage in decision-making processes that affect their growth and development. Teachers and students can cocreate classroom communities in which individuals are affirmed, enabled to belong, and taught social responsibility and social justice. It is a big job and worth every effort.

FOUR SOCIAL AND EMOTIONAL CONDITIONS FOR LEARNING

Based on the research done by the American Institutes for Research (AIR), there are four important social and emotional conditions for learning that can create this engaged community of learners,[53] which I have adapted to reflect how they can be effectively implemented in a HEART-filled classroom. These conditions illustrate the *what*—the necessary elements of a positive classroom climate. In the next chapter, we will dig deeper into the HEART skills and will explore the *how*—teaching and effectively infusing these skills into your teaching practice.

Physical, Emotional, and Intellectual SAFETY	Academic ENGAGEMENT and CHALLENGE
o Behavioral supports o Healthy boundaries o Identity safety	o High expectations o Academic mindsets o Student-centered instruction
SUPPORTS and CONNECTIONS	**SOCIAL, EMOTIONAL, and CULTURAL CAPACITY**
o Meaningful connections to peers and students o Sense of belonging o Effective supports	o HEART skills o Resilience o Shared ownership

PHYSICAL, EMOTIONAL, AND INTELLECTUAL SAFETY

Students feel physically, emotionally, and intellectually safe, and are treated equitably.

Fear and stress are not helpful emotions when it comes to learning. When we are scared, our amygdala activates, sending emergency signals to our brain and body so we can protect ourselves from danger. Fear also makes our thinking more rigid and shuts down the brain to exploration. Prolonged stressful situations impair our ability to learn and to maintain physical health. Although these emotions are part of our human experience, we want to create learning environments where students feel motivated, curious, and safe, which are better emotions for healthy growth and development.

When students feel physically, emotionally, and intellectually safe, their brains can fully open to new information, connections, and experiences. There are three things that you can do to help students feel safe in your classroom:

- Provide behavioral supports.

- Establish healthy boundaries.

- Create an identity safe space.

Provide behavioral supports. Behavior management is probably one of the most dreaded and painful aspects of teaching. Managing the social dynamics of a classroom and dealing with conflict are as much a part of teaching as lesson planning and writing report cards. One of the challenges I encountered as a teacher that I know is shared by many colleagues, was developing a positive and balanced discipline in my classroom, one in which I could consistently hold the line for healthy boundaries while nurturing a caring and supportive relationships with my students. This was tough. Although I had a vision for what I wanted my classroom to look and feel like, I was not always able to recreate that vision; I would react to students' disruptive behavior by providing an immediate consequence or I would rely too much on students with attentive behaviors. I was an effective teacher for many of my students—but not all—until I realized that students needed *behavior supports* as much as they needed help with fractions and solving multi-step problems. When I stopped thinking about classroom management as "discipline," and instead as providing students with intentional supports to help them make better choices, I not only felt better about my teaching but also became more effective at managing my class.

Reflect on your own experience. What is classroom discipline for you? Do you have positive role models that you would like to imitate? Did you have negative role models that influence how you respond to students' disruptive behaviors? If you see behavior as communication (for a review of this concept, see page 24), how can you use students' messages to support the development of their behavioral skill set?

Establish healthy boundaries. The other side of creating an environment where students feel physically and emotionally safe is setting up healthy boundaries. We can differentiate between two different types:

- *Nonnegotiables*: These are the classroom rules and limits that will be consistently protected for the sake of students' safety and to maintain a positive learning environment. These rules should be clear and fair to students and should be followed *consistently*. As you have probably experienced in your own teaching, consistency is a key point in ensuring that boundaries are enacted by students. When we change our expectations from day to day, the unintended message for students is that these rules are arbitrary or unfair. If you want to set up these limits with care while maintaining rich relationships with your students, create a plan for working with disruptions (it can be your own plan or one shared with other educators at your school). This will help you be more proactive and less reactive in your responses to students' behaviors. It also signals to students that you have the capacity to lead them in positive ways, even when holding them accountable.

- *Shared agreements*. These differ from nonnegotiable rules and limits, although they may overlap. Shared agreements are developed by students with guidance from the teacher. Students are involved in creating these agreements, which describe not only how they want to relate to each other in the classroom but also how they will respond if these agreements are broken. Shared agreements are a great tool for students in developing problem-solving skills and empathy for others. The process supports students in developing a sense of responsibility, ownership for the classroom community, and trust in their abilities to solve problems.

As with other aspects of teaching, setting up healthy boundaries and increasing students' positive behavior in class requires a good dose of introspection; we need to be curious about how we interpret students' behaviors and how we respond when they don't meet our expectations. Although it would be easier if we were able to be "fair" with all our students, the reality is that we, too, have blind spots and will make mistakes when managing students.

Research has shown that teachers' implicit bias not only impacts the expectations they hold regarding students' academic abilities, but also influences how and when they apply consequences for students' disruptive behaviors. In the US, Black students, boys, and students with disabilities are disproportionately disciplined in K-12 public schools, regardless of the type of disciplinary action, level of school poverty, or the type of school attended. For example, Black students accounted for 15.5 percent of all public school students but represented about 39 percent of students suspended from school—an overrepresentation of about 23 percentage points.[54]

Having a supportive approach to behavior expectations, rather than punitive, is an important component in creating a positive and welcoming classroom and in reducing the implicit bias many adults carry about students' behaviors. Even with a supportive environment, students and adults will make mistakes. Being able to acknowledge that mistakes are part of learning (not only in academics but also in the development of our social and emotional capacity) is a step in the right direction. And when harm has occurred, which will inevitably happen, things can be done to amend and repair.

Create an identity-safe space. Identity-safe environments value diversity by validating each individual's background and the multiple components of people's identities (age, race, gender, culture, language, sexual orientation). These are classrooms that work to eliminate the negative stereotypes used to define certain groups and where students don't need to hide or give up any part of themselves in order to be accepted. Many of the practices and HEART skills that we review in this book will help you support students to feel secure in their identities and, ultimately, free to be themselves. These practices contribute to building schools and classrooms where students have a sense of belonging and strong bonds with adults and peers.

ACADEMIC ENGAGEMENT AND CHALLENGE

Students experience challenging and engaging instruction.

A supportive classroom environment also incorporates productive instructional strategies that challenge and engage all students in the classroom, especially those who traditionally have been underserved by our current educational system, so they can be successful in college and beyond. As educators, our goal is to *increase the learning capacity of our students* by having high expectations for their learning, developing their academic mindsets, and putting them at the center of our curriculum and instructional practices. When we offer learning tasks that are appropriately challenging and engaging and we take the academic, social, and emotional needs of our students into consideration in the design of our classroom, we create rich soil for planting seeds that will bloom into meaningful learning. There are three things that you can do provide challenging and engaging instruction:

- Maintain high expectations.
- Help students develop academic mindsets.
- Develop student-centered instruction.

Maintain high expectations. Although progress has been made in serving BIPOC students in the US and around the globe, many culturally and linguistically diverse students still experience environments in which adults have low expectations for their academic performance. In a 2018 study of 4,000 students conducted by The New Teacher Project, an organization working to end educational inequality, almost 40 percent of classrooms made up mainly of students of color never handed out a single grade-level assignment, compared to only 12 percent of classrooms with mainly White students. Students of color were misled by inflated grades that suggested they were on track, even when they were not. Only 30 percent of students of color who earned an A in the Advanced Placement (AP) classes went on to pass their AP exam, compared to 78 percent of White students.[55]

The report also found that academic expectations of Black or Latinx students depended on a teacher's race; while 66 percent of teachers with the same race or ethnicity had high expectations for their students, that number dropped to 35 percent among teachers who did not share the same race or ethnicity, even when these students had the same levels of prior achievement.

In many cases, educators are not aware of this bias; it is unconscious, built in through sociocultural context and the way that certain groups are portrayed in the media. Although teachers may not hold lower expectations *intentionally*, research has shown that what teachers believe about their students' potential for academic success has a big impact on how students will perform.[56] When teachers hold high expectations for BIPOC students and/or who come from low-income families, students will rise to meet these expectations.

From a developmental perspective, if students are not challenged, they can become bored and disengaged. On the other hand, if students are asked to do work that is too difficult, they will most likely experience frustration and a high level of dependency on the educator's support. We know that emotions such as boredom, disengagement, and frustration don't open up the brain for learning, quite the opposite—they hinder students' ability to focus and fully engage.

From a practical perspective, educators can focus on what they can control and know how to do well—providing a high quality and rigorous academic program that holds students to high standards, while providing appropriate supports and scaffolding. When this happens, students learn that they are capable of high-level work.

Help students develop academic mindsets. Designing tasks that appropriately challenge students is also important because they influence students' perceptions about themselves as learners—children and youth form opinions about themselves based on their experiences with the material being taught. If the material is too difficult, they may doubt their skills and capacity to be successful. If the material is too easy, they may think that their teacher doesn't trust their abilities. Students' beliefs and attitudes have a powerful effect on their learning and achievement,[57] which is why effective teachers nurture positive academic mindsets in their classrooms as part of their academic instruction.

There are four key mindsets that have been identified as important for perseverance and academic success for students:

- Belief that one belongs in the school

- Belief in the value of the work

- Belief that effort will lead to increased competence

- A sense of self-efficacy and the ability to succeed[58]

When students develop these mindsets, they increase their self-concept and sense of affiliation to school, which results in higher levels of academic engagement. Although many of your students may not have these mindsets when they first come to your classroom, these beliefs are malleable and can be shaped over time. A good strategy for developing students' beliefs in their abilities—a growth mindset—is to provide feedback focused on effort and process (rather than prioritizing traits or final outcomes), and allow students opportunity for revision. Let mistakes be an important part of learning in your classroom! We will review how to incorporate these mindsets into classroom instruction in the next chapter.

Develop student-centered instruction. When students graduate from high school, they should be not only academically proficient but also socially and emotionally competent, so that they can be successful in higher education and prepared to enter the workplace. Today, the skills that employers are seeking differ from those that were relevant a decade ago; companies are looking for candidates who can problem solve, influence and inspire others, be comfortable with ambiguity, show persistence when faced with challenges, and be creative.

In order for students to develop these skills, they need a learning environment that is different from the one we (adults) experienced as students. Students will need a classroom where they can create content, work in groups to solve problems, research and present topics of interest, and present their learning in different ways. Those students who have learning gaps and/or have received poor instruction will need teachers who commit to accelerating their learning and teaching them how to learn.

Based on the science of learning and development, student-centered instruction can support students in developing the problem-solving and interpersonal skills needed for the twenty-first century.

Supporting students learning complex skills while providing scaffolding.	*Drawing on students' prior experiences and connecting with their lives.*
The zone of proximal development represents the learning space between what a student can do in a particular area and what they can do with some assistance. When educators provide well-designed instruction, they push students to new levels of understanding by providing supports that help them master new skills and advance their learning.	Students come to class with a diverse set of experiences, skills, knowledge, and interests. As educators, we can spark students' motivation for learning by contextualizing the content and making it relevant to students' lives. When students are able to bring what they already know into their classrooms, deeper connections can be made with the new academic content.
Creating rich environments for learning, including opportunities for collaboration with others.	*Providing cognitive supports.*
Learning is a social endeavor; we learn with and from others. Well-designed instruction incorporates opportunities for rich academic conversations and hands-on projects that support student learning.	This refers to using tools and strategies that help students make sense of the knowledge and skills they are learning. In some cases, educators will need to help students acquire background knowledge to access new content; in other cases, teachers focus on supporting students' independence and confidence by posting key informational posters around the classroom.

SUPPORTS AND CONNECTION

Students feel supported and connected to the world around them.

Meaningful classroom relationships impact students' growth and readiness for learning. Students need meaningful connections with adults in order to feel cared for and be motivated to learn. When students perceive that adults know them and are available to support them, they are more likely to engage in academic work, even when it is challenging. There are three things that you can do to help students feel supported and connected:

- Nurture meaningful connections to peers and adults.

- Create a sense of belonging.

- Provide effective supports.

Nurture meaningful connections to peers and adults. Children can thrive and develop a positive sense of self when they have positive relationships with their teachers and peers. As we have discussed, these meaningful connections impact the development of a healthy brain and serve as a protective factor for children who have experienced adversity. Students learn best when they can connect what happens in school to their prior experiences and when teachers are responsive to their particular needs. There are many things that you can do to establish meaningful connections with your students—creating an emotional bond, developing trust and being culturally responsive. For specific strategies, go back to Chapter Two in this book.

Create a sense of belonging. When teachers take the time to know their students well, they are better able to create productive learning opportunities for children and nurture a *sense of belonging* to the classroom community based on students' unique interests, talents, and skills. Community-building activities, consistent routines, personalized learning, and school-home partnerships are examples of practices that support these meaningful connections and a sense of belonging in the classroom. We'll review them in detail in the next chapter.

Provide effective supports. Creating the social and emotional conditions for all children's learning also means addressing students' individual needs that can create barriers to learning. These might be related to academic challenges, a lack of social and emotional skills, or adverse childhood experiences. To address children's needs, schools should provide a multitiered system of support that targets interventions based on students' individual learning trajectories. As you have probably experienced, students develop social, emotional, and academic skills at different rates, and they many need additional supports at certain times during their schooling. These supports are provided for as long a time as they are needed, but no longer, and generally include teams of teachers, families, and other professionals working together to better address students' needs.

SOCIAL AND EMOTIONAL CAPACITY

Students and adults are socially, emotionally, and culturally competent.

As we have noted, academic learning is highly connected with social and emotional competencies. Cognitive processes, such as problem-solving or decision-making, are tied to emotional skills, such as emotion recognition and management. The last 20 years of research in SEL has provided evidence of the need to explicitly teach these social and emotional competencies and infuse them into the everyday practice of educators and schools. The ultimate goal is to grow students and adults who are socially, emotionally, and culturally competent, which you can make possible by doing these three things:

- Teach and integrate HEART skills.

- Build resilience.

- Create shared ownership.

Teach and integrate HEART skills. The HEART in Mind model makes it possible to create the social and emotional conditions for learning in practical and meaningful ways, with five different skills aligned with the CASEL framework:

Honor Your Emotions

Elect Your Responses

Apply Empathy

Reignite Your Relationships

Transform with Purpose

As you practice and teach these HEART skills, and integrate them into your teaching, you will be growing the social and emotional capacity of your students and also contributing to an environment conducive to deeper learning. As we have discussed, SEL is not a behavior management system, but a process for equipping students with the skills they need for the 21st century and creating rich and supportive learning environments that serve the needs of all learners.

Build resilience. In this process, it is just as important that you pay attention to your own social and emotional capacity for three reasons:

- First, it would be hard to teach something that you don't practice yourself. In order to teach these skills with confidence, you need to develop fluency with the skills—what they mean, how they look in practice, how you use them for academic work, and how you knew when you "got" them. It is also necessary to learn how to unpack your bias and develop cultural competence, so you can best facilitate this learning for your students.

- Second, these skills support your *resilience* and well-being as an educator; they help you notice when you are feeling overwhelmed and recognize when you need some support.

- Third, these skills also help you connect with your purpose and the reasons why you do what you do on a daily basis. These skills can help you (re)engage with doing the work that matters. I will be discussing these three elements—voice, resilience, and purpose—in part three of this book, "The Whole-Hearted Educator."

Create shared ownership. A classroom that incorporates these HEART skills should be founded on students and educators working together to build this positive environment for everybody. This shared ownership means that the members of the classroom see themselves as active contributors, making decisions about their learning, holding each other accountable, and being responsible for maintaining a respectful and engaging class.

You can create the social and emotional conditions for a HEART-filled classroom by making sure that students feel physically, emotionally, and intellectually safe, are engaged and motivated to learn, have an appropriate level of support, and develop a sense of belonging.

When students and adults learn and practice their HEART skills, they build their resilience to face the challenges ahead through meaningful connections and shared ownership. Our role as educators is to cocreate this "container" for exploration, connectedness and growth with and for our students.

Endnotes

51 Hammond, Zaretta. *Culturally Responsive Teaching and the Brain: Promoting Authentic Engagement and Rigor Among Culturally and Linguistically Diverse Students.* Thousand Oaks, CA: Corwin, 2014.

52 Turner, Bret. "Teaching Kindness Isn't Enough." *Teaching Tolerance* 63, Fall 2019. https://www.tolerance.org/magazine/fall-2019/teaching-kindness-isnt-enough?fbclid=IwAR1aCXaT-gLI5aeRJCoYAKWdXMOhGs0BItrpQxBJ0w7ZR-qaNyPPBBfVGsho.

53 Osher, D., and Kimberly Kendziora. "Building conditions for learning and healthy adolescent development: A strategic approach." January 2010.

54 Nowicki, Jaqueline M., "K-12 Education: Discipline Disparities for Black Students, Boys, and Students with Disabilities. Report to Congressional Requesters." US Government Accountability Office. March 2018. https://files.eric.ed.gov/fulltext/ED590845.pdf.

55 Cantor, David. "America's Achievement Gap – Made, Not Born? What a Study of 30,000 Students Reveals." The New Teachers Projects (TNTP). September 25, 2018. https://tntp.org/news-and-press/view/americas-achievement-gap-made-not-born-what-a-study-of-30000-students-revea.

56 Turner, Julianne C., Andrea Christensen, and Debra K. Meyer. "Teachers' Belief About Student Learning and Motivation." In *International Handbook of Research on Teachers and Teaching*, vol. 21, edited by L. J. Saha and A. G. Dworkin. https://doi.org/10.1007/978-0-387-73317-3_23.

57 Darling-Hammond, Linda, and Channa Cook-Harvey. "Educating the Whole Child: Improving School Climate to Support Success." Learning Policy Institute. September 7, 2018. https://learningpolicyinstitute.org/product/educating-whole-child-report.

58 Farrington, Camille A., "Academic Mindsets as a Critical Component of Deeper Learning." University of Chicago. April 2013.

Chapter 5: Teaching and Integrating the HEART in Mind Model

> *"We have so many pressures, and we feel the need to push our kids and have them grow. There are a lot of extrinsic forces at play. (SEL) it is a great reminder that first and foremost we need to be nurturing our kids and making sure they are growing emotionally."[59]*
>
> — *Teacher, East Palo Alto (California)*

Most educators—such as the one quoted above—believe that it is important to teach SEL; they realize that students cannot focus academically if they are experiencing strong emotions or are constantly stressed. Yet, given time constraints and academic pressure, many teachers struggle to find ways to incorporate this work in their teaching. The challenges of effective and sustainable implementation cannot be ignored.

Several teachers in my research expressed *feeling guilty* about stopping their academic instruction to deal with social and emotional issues. They were concerned about falling behind in their scope and sequence and then not being able to catch up.[60]

However, when these teachers included SEL time in their daily schedule, they realized they now had a *common language* for discussing social and emotional issues with students, making these conversations more effective. At the same time, they started to see students self-monitoring more often and solving problems on their own, which meant they didn't need as much support and facilitation from the teacher. Teachers reported that the benefits of teaching these skills outgrew the challenges they had to overcome to make them work in their classrooms.

What are the HEART skills students need in order to successfully engage in your classroom?

Effective teachers know when and how to introduce certain academic skills and/or content in their classrooms. They provide opportunities to connect with prior knowledge, they teach and create activities for guided practice, they have students decide how they will show their learning. They are clear on students' starting points and where they should be once they are done. However, sometimes teachers misjudge in considering the *HEART skills* that students need to put into practice in order to engage with the academic content and participate in all these activities.

For example, think about a pair-share activity where students have to solve a mathematical word problem together. You may have students who are eager to share their thinking, while others may be more reluctant. How can you ensure that all students can participate in the activity on equal terms? You could provide students with an opportunity to:

- Explore their feelings about solving mathematical problems or working in pairs, which would be related to Honor Your Emotions.

- Review what active listening looks and feels like, which would be related to Reignite Your Relationships.

- Discuss a tool that would help them share the speaking time equally, which would be related to Elect Your Responses.

While teaching HEART skills explicitly is a key component of a robust SEL intervention, it is not the only one. Using teaching practices that enhance students' use of HEART skills and infusing SEL with the academic content you teach are two additional strategies for making the most out of your SEL implementation. When you consider the HEART skills that students need in order to access and master the content taught in your classroom, and you work to teach and infuse them in your practice, you are providing students with the tools they need to learn and grow.

THREE IMPLEMENTATION STRATEGIES

1. **Explicit instruction of HEART skills.** This strategy refers to teaching the specific skills and vocabulary in the HEART in Mind model. When starting to teach SEL, explicit instruction is very powerful because it provides students and educators with a common language to communicate and discuss daily issues in and outside the classroom. Educators may want to use other SEL-related resources, such as Common Sense Media or Teaching Tolerance, and develop their own lessons and activities. The key here is knowing *what* you will be teaching, before you can decide how you will do it.

2. **Teaching practices that enhance students' HEART skills.** This strategy is directly tied to how you organize and manage your classroom. Instructional practices that require students to work and learn together, discuss a topic, collect different points of view, solve a math or science problem in a small group, or to make choices about their own learning are activities that ask students to use HEART skills in one way or another. Although these strategies are often used in schools, they are not thought of as resources for developing students' social and emotional capacity. To make sure you are consistent with your explicit instruction, you should inform students *which* competencies they are practicing and developing when they participate in these activities. A few examples of teaching practices that enhance students' competencies include cooperative learning, classroom discussions, project-based learning, workshops, feedback loops, and student self-assessment.

3. **Integrating HEART skills with academic content.** This third strategy connects the content and vocabulary of your HEART instruction with your English, math, science, or physical education lesson. For example, in language arts it's possible to connect lessons and activities around the study of characters or the development of themes

with emotional literacy and self-management skills. As we have not-ed earlier, educators should include both an academic and a HEART objective in their lessons plans, and share them with students.

On the following pages, you will find an implementation roadmap for teaching and integrating the HEART in Mind model in your classroom. For each of the HEART skills, I have provided the following information:

- Definition: This includes a description of its meaning, the research that backs its importance, and often an illustrative story.

- Key Concepts: This includes subskills or essential components to help you understand the scope of the particular HEART skill.

- Indicators of Mastery: This includes specific benchmarks by grade level.

- Classroom Application: This includes the activities, strategies, and tools that you can implement in your classroom to help your students develop each HEART skill. It is organized following the three implementation strategies reviewed earlier—direct instruction, integration with teaching practices, and integration with academic content. In Chapter Six, you will find tips and additional activities for implementing these skills in a virtual classroom.

You may be tempted to skip the definition and key concepts, and go straight to the tips for teaching and infusing it in your classroom. Don't give in to the temptation! These sections provide the basic principles and key knowledge that will make you more effective in teaching the HEART in Mind model.

By teaching these HEART skills and infusing them with your teaching practices and academic content, you are maximizing the impact of your implementation and creating an environment where students have a desire to learn and the tools to thrive.

H—HONOR YOUR EMOTIONS

Definition

Honoring your emotions means naming, interpreting, and appropri-ately communicating feelings.

Two years ago, I got an email from my daughter's kindergarten teacher. My daughter had kicked two boys in the groin that morning at school, and the teacher wanted to schedule a meeting. When I finished reading the email my heart was beating fast and my cheeks had flushed. I sat at my desk in disbelief. "I cannot believe she did this! What is going on with her?" I thought, trying to manage my emotions. As I sat with my feelings for a bit longer, I realized that I had mixed emotions about this situation:

I felt *upset* and thought, "What was she thinking? Why did she do something like this?"

I felt *ashamed* and thought, "What am I doing wrong? I spend all this time trying to help teachers with SEL, and this is not getting through to my child!"

But under those feelings, there were others, hiding. I felt worried and scared; maybe she was having issues in school and hadn't told me. Maybe she was being bullied and felt the need to fight back. Maybe . . . .

That evening, I had a conversation with my daughter about this situation. I was glad that I'd had time to process my *own* emotions before having this conversation. *If we move too quickly through our emotions, we can miss not only the information they're communicating but also the depth and variety of our own feelings.*

When we honor our emotions, we are able to use emotion words to describe our feelings—I felt upset and ashamed about my daughter's actions—and reflect on the meaning of these feelings, so we can constructively express them to others. The action verb in this skill—*honor*—refers to approaching our feelings with respect and treating them as friends with important messages, rather than as enemies that we need to fight. This is an important skill for increasing self-awareness and developing a stronger sense of confidence, and it is a building block for the rest of the skills in the HEART in Mind model.

Key Concepts

Honoring your emotions entails being able to do the following:

1. ***Naming emotions.*** The first aspect of honoring emotions is developing our *emotional literacy*, so we can better label what we feel.

Many children and youth express being happy, sad, or mad, but miss the subtle gradations in emotions because they don't have the words to describe them. Accurately naming emotions helps students to be clearer about what is happening inside, so they can manage themselves in positive ways and become better learners. When students increase their vocabulary for describing emotions, they are developing a more nuanced understanding of themselves, their relationships, and the world around them.

As a first step, help students connect their feelings with their bodily sensations:

- Tightness in the throat when feeling scared

- A knot in the stomach when nervous

- Rapid heartbeat when upset

- Blushing when embarrassed

As students start developing this skill, they realize that sometimes they experience more than one emotion at a time:

– I am *proud* of the science project I just finished and *scared* that my friends might make fun of it.

– I feel *nervous* about meeting my new soccer teammates and *excited* to start the soccer season again.

– I am *upset* that my brother took my bike and *afraid* he might break it.

Emotional literacy also helps students identify the *degree of intensity* in different emotions and how they change over time if we don't do anything to regulate them—annoyance becomes anger, anger becomes fury. This will help students (and adults) manage their emotions as they start to develop their capacity to look within and identify their feelings.

Intensity of Emotions

ENRAGED	DEPRESSED
FURIOUS	HOPELESS
ANGRY	**SAD**
IRRITATED	GLOOMY
ANNOYED	PENSIVE

ECSTATIC	HYSTERICAL
EXCITED	TERRIFIED
HAPPY	**AFRAID**
CHEERFUL	APPREHENSIVE
AT EASE	WORRIED

FRANTIC	WORTHLESS
DISTURBED	DEFICIENT
ANXIOUS	**INADEQUATE**
NERVOUS	UNABLE
IMPATIENT	UNCERTAIN

2. ***Interpreting emotions.*** The next skill is being able to *understand why* we have these feelings and the events that activate them. This is sometimes difficult for students to do; it requires understanding how emotions can help them. For example, anger can help us fight against problems, like when we get upset if the rules of the game are not followed. Or sadness may allow us to connect with those we love, when our pet dies and the family comes together to cuddle. It is important to communicate that all feelings are helpful, even the ones that cause us to be uncomfortable!

Marco was doing some measurements in the classroom for a math lesson. The teacher said students needed to finish their work that afternoon or they would have to take it home and finish it, because the next day each student would present their work. Marco didn't want to take the work home that afternoon because he was going to the movies with his father. He was trying hard to get the problem done.

After leaving his desk for a minute to grab some materials, he came back and the measuring tape was gone. He looked around and saw Jessica with *his* measuring tape. He walked up to her and said, "Hey, give me that. I was using it." When Jessica didn't hand him the measuring tape, Marco pushed her to the floor, grabbed it from her hands, and walked back to his desk to finish the work.

When the teacher called on Marco to find out what happened, Marco was able to say he was upset because Jessica took the measuring tape he was using. When asked why he pushed Jessica to the floor, he responded that he was trying to finish his work and needed the measuring tape. Since this behavior was not common for Marco, the teacher kept prompting him until they got to the bottom of the situation: it was very important for Marco to finish his work at school so he could enjoy a special time with his father without having to do any schoolwork at home.

The conversation with the teacher helped Marco realize why he was so upset with Jessica. It was partly because she took something he needed, but mostly it was because she got in the way of something he really wanted—going to the movies with his father. Marco walked to Jessica's desk and asked: "Are you okay? I am sorry that I pushed you and grabbed the tape from your hands."

If we want students to develop their capacity to interpret emotions, we need to become *emotion coaches* and help them see not just what's on the surface but also the underlying cause of their feelings, and how these emotions drive our actions. These are some prompts that may help you to support students with this process:

- What happened?

- How did that make you feel? What else were you feeling?

- What is this feeling telling you about the situation?

- Why is this feeling happening now?

When you are supporting a child who is experiencing strong emotions or has made a poor choice, be respectful of their experience and show empathy. Remember that behavior is communication, especially when the behavior is not appropriate. Validate their feelings so they know it is okay to have those emotions. Then, address the behavior as needed. How can the student repair the harm inflicted?

It is normal for children and youth to lose their emotional balance at times. Once they are able to reflect on the situation, guide them toward identifying the underlying cause. If this is a recurring feeling and reaction for the student, brainstorm together to identify ways to respond the next time this emotion arises.

3. ***Appropriately communicating emotions.*** Another aspect of honoring our emotions is learning ways to appropriately express them. Ignoring or suppressing our feelings does not make them go away, and they may show up later in unexpected ways. At the other end of the spectrum, you may have students who overexpress their emotions; this may be a sign that they haven't yet learned how to process these feelings on their own and may need your support to do so. Overexpressing emotions can impact a person's ability to maintain

positive and healthy relationships in the long term. The key here is to find the appropriate *balance* between our internal processing (recognizing, naming, and interpreting our feelings) and the external expression (how much, where, and with whom we share).

There are a few things you should consider in supporting students in this area:

- *We have different expectations of boys and girls.* Although boys are wired to tune into their feelings just as much as girls, parents tend to encourage their daughters to share their feelings far more than they do their sons. Boys are told, "Cover up your emotions," "Be tough." In her book *Unselfie: Why Empathetic Kids Succeed in Our All-About-Me World*, Dr. Michelle Borba explains that parents are apt to discuss more emotional experiences with girls, while with boys they leave out crucial clues that may help them learn emotional literacy.[61] For example, while parents may point out emotional situations and discuss those experiences with girls ("Look at that little girl; she is crying because she doesn't want to leave the park and go back home."), parents of boys may discuss the causes and consequences of expressing emotions ("If your friends see you crying, won't they make fun of you?"). Although parents are starting to realize the unintended consequences of the ways in which we raise girls and boys, gender norms about emotional expression continue to impact how much (or how little) students share about their emotions in the classroom.

- *Cultural backgrounds and family values influence how we express emotions.* Although many families don't have "family rules" when it comes to expressing emotions, these are communicated in subtle ways.[62] For example, imagine a parent storming out of the room every time a child is upset. The child may interpret that to mean that anger is not an acceptable emotion and may try to suppress it in the future. In other families, it may be normal to have conversations about feelings.

In this case, it will be important for the teacher to know and understand students' prior experience and to guide them toward determining ways of expressing emotions that are appropriately aligned with their cultural values and the school's context.

4. *Approaching emotions with no judgment*. As previously mentioned, emotions are data; they can provide valuable information that can help us make better decisions. At the same time, if we don't have tools to process them, emotions can be confusing and make us feel out of control. Children and youth may feel the need to avoid the strong emotions that make us feel uncomfortable: fear, anger, embarrassment. But the reality is, there's no way to avoid our feelings. In fact, it's good and healthy for kids to feel and express these feelings. An important message in teaching students to honor their emotions is this: there is nothing wrong with having these emotions; feelings are not good or bad, they are just information.

This is something that adults often forget. Imagine a child sharing that she is nervous about the upcoming gymnastics competition with her coach. The coach looks at her with a smile and says, "Don't be nervous, everything will be fine. I will be there with you." Although the coach's intention is to comfort the child, he is invalidating her feelings. As in the earlier example where the parent left the room when the kid was upset, this child may be learning that she *shouldn't* feel nervous. A better way to respond to the child would be, "I understand you are nervous. It's okay. If I were competing, I would probably be nervous too. Do you remember when we had the Fall Festival? You were nervous then too, right? Do you recall what you did to calm down? Oh, you took some deep breaths. That's a great strategy. Would you like us to do it together? I will be there with you."

Validating the child's experience is a key part of this process, as we want children and youth to regularly tune in to their emotions. If we judge how kids feel ("You shouldn't feel that way"), they will be less likely to develop their emotional literacy and ability to manage their emotions. Validate first, then help them cope and process the emotion. Finally, support them in interpreting and communicating.

1. **Identify and name the emotion:**	I am feeling so nervous.
2. **Validate the emotion:**	It is okay. It is normal to feel nervous before a big event.
3. **Process the emotion:**	I am going to take a few deep breaths to feel a bit calmer.
4. **Interpret the emotion:**	I am feeling so nervous because this event is very important to me and my family. It's an indication that I care.
5. **Communicate the emotion:**	Coach, I am feeling very nervous. Can we take a few breaths together?

Indicators of Mastery

Beginner (kindergarten through second grade)

- Uses a variety of emotion words

- Connects emotions with bodily sensations

- Describes how emotions are linked to behavior

Advanced Beginner (third through fifth grade)

- Describes a range of emotions

- Identifies the reasons behind their emotions

- Expresses how they feel to others

Strategic Learner (sixth to eighth grade)

- Recognizes the different degrees of intensity in their emotions

- Identifies the complexity and meaning of feelings

- Demonstrates when and how feelings can be communicated appropriately

Emerging Expert (ninth through 12th grade)

- Analyzes factors that create difficult emotions, such as stress or fear

- Generates ways to interpret and communicate emotions

- Applies strategies to use emotions effectively

Practicing Expert (college and beyond)

- Identifies how emotions affect decision-making and interprets their meaning

- Evaluates how expressing emotions affects others and communicates accordingly

- Generates ways to use emotions to accomplish personal goals

CLASSROOM APPLICATION

There are many ways to help children develop their emotional literacy and their ability to interpret and express emotions—creating a feelings word wall, identifying the emotions of the characters in the stories students read, sharing how we feel during classroom meetings. No matter what grade level or academic subject you teach, there are practical ways to help kids honor their emotions. Figure out what works for you and your students!

Direct Instruction

Create a "map" of where emotions are felt in the body. Help students find the connection between their emotions and physical sensations in their bodies by asking, "What do you notice in your body when you are___?" On poster board, draw a body and ask students to name some emotions they know. As students suggest emotions, ask them to think about where they feel them in the body. Have students put their hands there (the stomach, the throat, the heart). You can also have students create their own individual map. This activity is especially useful for students who regularly experience intense emotions and those who move quickly from being calm to being furious. When students pay attention to their body sensations, they are more likely to become aware of their emotions.

Teach how the brain works. In their book *The Whole-Brain Child*, Dr. Daniel J. Siegel and Dr. Tina Payne Bryson suggest a simple way to understand and explain how the brain works. Picturing the brain like a house, you can identify the downstairs brain—the limbic system—where important things live that keep us safe and take care of our needs: strong emotions that keep us out of danger, our reactions of fight-flight-freeze if we are under threat. In the upstairs brain—the neocortex—complex things happen: thinking, planning, problem-solving. The upstairs brain is not fully formed until we reach our mid-20s! In order to be a healthy, functioning person, we need to use both the downstairs and upstairs brain. Adapt the language to your students' age so they can understand and use that language to describe their reactions. For older students, you can make it a research project, where they have to find out more information about their brains and how they work.

Do emotional check-ins. An emotional check-in is a time when students and teachers come together to connect and reflect on how things are going. Students are encouraged to share how they feel with the group or maybe a partner. You can use cards with faces that show different emotions and have students point to the face that matches their feeling. Then, you can help them find the appropriate word. If students already have an emotion vocabulary, they can share aloud. If you have a "feelings word wall" in the classroom, encourage students to use different words to describe their emotions. Share how you feel as well. *Modeling is important in increasing students' social and emotional skills.*

Create a feelings word wall. You can get it started by brainstorming all the emotion words your students know. During your classroom meeting or advisory period, ask students to generate new feeling words and review the old ones. What other emotion words can be added? When students do a writing assignment, encourage them to use words from the feelings word wall.

Play feeling charades. Have students write the names of a few emotions on index cards. Each student pulls a card and acts out the emotion using his face and body, but with no sounds or words. The goal is to guess the person's emotion. For younger students, use basic emotions (sad, happy, angry), and as students expand their vocabulary, challenge them to guess other emotions (confused, hopeful, relived). Make it playful and have fun!

Integration with Teaching Practices

Transitions. Adjusting the energy level from recess to being back in the physical or virtual classroom or adapting to different behavior expectations from math class to Spanish can be challenging for students. Even switching activities in the elementary classroom can be difficult for certain learners. Use these transitions to help students connect with their feelings. If you are starting a lesson with a new group, take a minute to have them record their emotions in a journal or notebook at the beginning of the class. You can also set up 10 cups, numbered one to 10, and have students place a popsicle stick in the cup that reflects how they feel: one (worst day of their life) to 10 (best day ever). You can discuss the overall results with the class or just use this information in your teaching. If most of the students pick numbers on the lower side of the scale, you may consider taking a few minutes to discuss what is happening before you start the lesson. The key here is to help students connect with their emotions so they can prepare for new learning. This is especially important if you are teaching virtually—students' emotions impact their predisposition for learning.

Beginning and ending your lesson. The start of a lesson is an important time for creating interest and stimulating students' curiosity. Use tools that will *hook* your students from the beginning: a short video, a compelling story, a powerful question, or an enticing visual. The emotions students experience during this time are an important part of a successful lesson. Ask yourself, "What emotions do I want students to experience during this time? What are the tools I will use to generate these emotions?"

The end of a lesson or period is an important time for students to make sense of their learning. However, in many cases, teachers skip the reflection part of the lesson plan because they run out of time. While it is understandable, it is not serving students well. In order for students to *apply* what they have learned in the classroom, they need the time to reflect and process the content and/or skills from the lesson. This is also a way to bring closure to that period and prepare students for their next activity. You can use classroom discussions, individual journals, or exit tickets to help students reflect on their learning. Here are some prompts that may be helpful (adapt them as needed based on your students' ages):

o   What was the learning objective for this lesson/project?

o   Which part of this lesson/project did you enjoy the most? Why?

o   Which part of this lesson/project did you enjoy the least? Why?

o   What did you learn from this lesson/project?

o   What are you looking forward to learning in this class?

Challenging tasks and projects. As educators, we cannot protect students from ever experiencing feelings of failure and disappointment when doing class work. In fact, as we have discussed, it is healthy for students to wrestle with these emotions in a supportive environment. However, educators can create an environment where *it is okay* to have these feelings, and where students have the tools to process them and try again. In many cases, students have limiting beliefs about their abilities to succeed, which impacts their performance and how they react in the face of challenge. Being presented with a challenging task is exhilarating for some students and terrifying for others. What is the difference? Having a growth mindset, which is believing their ability and competence can grow with their effort. This is important for teachers, because academic mindsets can be more of a factor in holding students back from learning than their knowledge or skills.[63] To support your students:

o   Explore with your students their beliefs about their ability to do challenging tasks.

o   Welcome mistakes as a normal part of the learning process in your classroom. Do it explicitly and recognize when you make mistakes too.

o   Allow students to acknowledge how they feel about tackling challenging tasks.

Integration with Academic Instruction

Language arts. Language instruction—English or any other language—is a great place to integrate discussions about emotions and to further develop the first skill in the HEART model: Honor Your Emotions. Many educational standards, such as the English-Language Arts Common Core Standards in the US, are naturally aligned with social and emotional skills. For example:

o Third grade, Reading Literature: Describe characters in a story (e.g., their traits, motivations, or feelings) and explain how their actions contribute to the sequence of events.

o Sixth grade, Reading Literature: Describe how a story's or drama's plot unfolds in a series of episodes as well as how the characters respond or change as the plot moves toward a resolution.

o Eighth grade, Reading Literature: Analyze how particular lines of dialogue or incidents in a story or drama propel the action, reveal aspects of a character, or provoke a decision.

If you teach in the US and your state has not adopted Common Core, or if you teach in a different country, look for those standards that ask students to analyze characters and how stories unfold. When you teach those standards, you will be helping students identify emotions, therefore supporting their emotional literacy.

Can your students use a wide variety of emotion words to describe the character's feelings? Can they provide evidence about *why* they think the character was feeling that way (body language, tone of voice, action that was taken)? What was the message of that emotion? Remember that the hardest aspect of honoring emotions is interpreting their message. Six Seconds, the global network of EQ practitioners, calls this "wisdom of feelings." Literary fiction is a great tool for engaging students in discussions about the meaning of emotions and how characters can use them to make decisions. If you create a feelings word wall, you can add emotions to it as you read different books. If you don't have a feelings wall, use the books you read in class to get the discussion started. Help students make the connection between emotions and (re)actions. What were the pros and cons of the characters' actions? This type of question will help students develop their consequential thinking.

History. Teaching history offers a great opportunity for teachers and students to confront the complexities of humanity in ways that promote critical thinking, empathy, and moral development. When you equip students with the language to discuss emotions, you are setting up the foundation to have difficult conversations about topics such as racism, immigration, diversity, or human rights. This happens first, by recognizing how we feel when others disagree with our opinions; second, by learning how figures like Nelson Mandela and Martin Luther King, Jr., used their strong emotions for positive change. Organizations such as Teaching Tolerance or Facing History and Ourselves are great resources for incorporating HEART skills into history lessons.

Music. The history of music is full of artists who struggled to find a place in the music scene, were often broke, and sometimes lost hope that they would ever make it. Ask students about their favorite musicians and help them analyze these artists under the lens of social and emotional competencies. Another way to integrate SEL in your music class is by analyzing songs through emotional literacy. I cannot think of a place where you can identify more emotions and feelings than in music—with or without lyrics. You can also discuss how music makes students feel and how different genres might generate similar or different emotions. Music is often therapeutic for many of us, so try discussing how music can be used to increase motivation or engage optimism with your students. Incorporating music recommended by our students is also a way to be culturally responsive.

Mathematics. The Common Core State Standards in mathematics reflect the view that *learning is a social process,* implicitly calling for teaching practices that leverage the power of group work and collaborative learning. The Standards for Mathematical Practice (known as SMPs) require that students solve real-world problems by working effectively with peers: elaborating and communicating arguments; understanding and critiquing diverse points of view; and persevering in solving problems. Those skills seem to go beyond being able to fill out some bubble sheets, right? In order to develop students who are mathematically proficient in the Common Core standards, math instruction needs to incorporate the development of social and emotional competencies. Here's an example:

Standards for Mathematical Practice 1: Make sense of problems and persevere in solving them.

Expectations	Students' Work	Connection to HEART skills
Students will make sense of the information in a problem through different approaches. Students will identify alternative ways to solve complex problems.	Students will try to explain the meaning of the problem and look for entry points to the solution. They will find different pathways to solve the problem using a variety of tools: concrete objects, graphs, pictures, etc. Students will check their answers and continually ask, "Does this make sense?" They will be able to explain the different approaches and why/how they are relevant.	**H-Honor Your Emotions:** Students will need to know their strengths, determine what they know about the topic, and connect with their initial emotions to engage with the content. **E-Elect Your Responses:** Students will need to regulate their behavior and avoid distractions. They'll need to monitor their progress, considering time and effort to meet their goal.

Honoring emotions can help students develop stronger mathematics skills. As we discussed in Chapter One, students may have different feelings about this content area based on their perceived ability, gender, the race-based social stereotypes related to math they may have internalized, their personal interest, and their prior experience with this area. To support your students:

o **Discuss your students' emotional reaction to math problems with them.** Do they get excited about the subject or shut down? What's their stress level in your class? If the emotions generated by the subject are not conducive to productive work, you will need to offer alternative ways to think about the subject. How is math connected with the outside world? How can math help them meet their goals or the things they care about? This is a great discussion that brings to life the skill of Honoring Your Emotions.

o **Share your own feelings about math and model how you prepare yourself to do the work:** "When I have to solve this kind of problem, I feel _____. Then, I tell myself, 'You can do it, just take it one step at a time.'"

o **Help students identify their strengths.** This is the foundation of self-awareness! Students who can identify their strengths will be more likely to build on them to improve their areas of growth. They will probably have greater motivation and will be more self-confident.

Tools for Measurement

In the appendix of this book, you will find a table with the indicators of mastery for each HEART skill. This scope and sequence can help you identify areas where your students need additional support. You will also find a self-assessment survey to help you reflect on your own HEART skills.

E—ELECT YOUR RESPONSES

Definition

Electing your responses means creating space to make constructive and safe decisions.

Elect Your Responses teaches students and adults the tools to create the necessary space that allow us to make constructive, informed, and safe decisions. The action verb in this skill—elect—means to *choose*, to take the reins of our behavior and select how we are going to move forward. The word "responses" means that we move away from reactions and functioning on autopilot, and step into a place of balance. Let me illustrate.

Olivia was a middle school student at a large school where I supported teachers with their SEL practices. Olivia was very opinionated, as many middle school students are, and seemed to feel angry often; in class, she would argue with students about big and small things and she publicly criticized her teachers. She was often perceived as defiant and was sent to the principal's office on a regular basis—she had a difficult time processing her anger before speaking out.

Olivia's teachers expected her to "get over" whatever she was feeling and just focus on learning. They assumed she was too old to be taught about emotional literacy or how to take a deep breath. Her teachers shared with me that they did not have time to be Olivia's personal therapist. They needed to focus on content so they could finish teaching the class standards before the end of the school year.

There are two independent but related things happening in this situation:

    a. Olivia struggles to regulate her anger. When she feels angry, she expresses it by arguing, criticizing, or displaying defiant behavior. She gets sent to the office in response to inappropriate behavior, which moves the issue outside the classroom but does not resolve her challenges with regulating her emotions.

    b. Olivia's teachers perceive that it is not their role to help Olivia learn how to process her anger. This is something she should have learned already. They are busy trying to finish their content and don't want to provide the individualized attention this student requires.

Although these teachers may have been right that Olivia needed additional support, they had two misconceptions about social and emotional skills, the first being that students are able to "get over" their emotions. While this may be true for certain students, it is not accurate for all. Some of the students in our classrooms need additional support to (re)gain their emotional balance. The same way that students may need additional academic support at some point in their schooling, they may also need additional social and emotional support. Many elementary schools do not yet incorporate an intentional focus on SEL, which leaves students with fewer tools to regulate their emotions in the middle and high school years. No matter which grade span you teach, do not underestimate how much you can do to support students' social and emotional growth.

When we ignore students' emotions or expect them to go away, we are denying students' experiences and ignoring their value. Remember, you can help students experiencing strong emotions by connecting with their feelings. Acknowledge and validate: "Your face is tense, you seem upset." "What happened?" "I might also feel upset if that happened to me."

The second misconception held by Olivia's teachers was in regard to students' ability to learn self-management skills; it is never too late to learn tools to process our emotions, especially for students whose feelings are getting in the way of learning. When students feel out of control due to their emotions, they cannot and will not learn—no matter how well-designed your lesson might be. Our job as educators is, as Dr. Daniel Siegel says, to "co-regulate," that is, to help students regain emotional balance and to increase their capacity to regulate their feelings, so they can see things more clearly and respond to daily situations instead of reacting, as Olivia was doing.

Key Concepts

Electing Your Responses entails being able to do the following:

1. **Managing emotions**

   Dealing with uncomfortable emotions, such as anger, is not an easy task—for kids or for adults. While anger is a basic human emotion that can provide great energy for solving problems, if we don't manage it constructively, it can have disastrous consequences in our lives and for our relationships. **When we are angry, we tend to react instead of responding to the situation.** This reaction, and not the emotion itself, is generally what creates trouble. The goal of managing emotions is not to eliminate these feelings but to process them *before* we take action so that we can create value through them. Remember that the prefrontal cortex is still developing during childhood and adolescence, which makes it harder for kids and teenagers to remain in control of their emotions and behaviors. However, we can support their development and teach them additional tools to increase their capacity to manage their behavior in positive ways.

One strategy that I have found works really well for children and youth is a visual that shows the different zones a person can experience at any given moment. Some models have three zones, but I like to use the four-color model.

Red zone	This is when young people and adults experience intense fear, anger, frustration, or disappointment. The nervous system takes over and the person cannot handle the demands of the situation at that particular time. Some students may lash out, yell, and become physically or verbally aggressive. The red-zone response is outward.
Yellow zone	This is when young people and adults experience less intense emotions such as excitement, silliness, annoyance, or anxiety. The person remains in control and is able to monitor their behavior.
Green zone	This is when young people and adults are in a place of balance, where the young person or adult is calm and regulated. The person feels in control and can handle the situation.
Blue zone	This is when young people and adults experience emotions such as disappointment, sadness, or boredom. They respond to these emotions by shutting down and moving inward.

This visual helps students monitor their feelings. Leah Kuypers, author of *The Zones of Regulation*, compares the zones to traffic signs.[64] The red zone is similar to finding a stop sign on the road: emotions are taking control; there is a need to pause and manage these emotions before taking any action. A yellow sign means that you can proceed, but with caution. That is the case for the yellow zone; although individuals are still in control of their behavior, they may need to use a strategy to process their feelings and avoid escalating to the red zone. Or they may need to adjust their behavior if they change context, such as in regulating their energy level as they move from recess to the classroom. When students are in the green zone, that means the way is clear and they can go. Finally, the blue zone can be compared to a rest area, when there is a need to refuel.

In his parenting book *The Yes Brain*, Dr. Daniel J. Siegel argues that when students have a *wide* green zone, they are able to experience frustration, sadness, or fear while still keeping their emotional balance and remaining in the green zone. They can tolerate a broad range of emotional experiences and are balanced and adaptable.

The key here is to help students move back quickly to the green zone and expand its width over time. How do you think having a visual with the zones of regulation would help Olivia manage her emotions? What other tools do you think might help her to widen her green zone? In the Direct Instruction section of this skill, you will find a list of strategies that you can teach your students to help them widen their green zones.

2. **Identifying triggers and patterns to see our choices more clearly**

If you have been teaching for a while, you can probably recall students who had intense reactions to certain situations: the student who shut down when a mistake was pointed out to him or the student who got angry at her friends if they did not want to play soccer during recess. Students' nervous systems automatically respond to daily events based on different factors, including past experiences, the current situation, or the student's innate temperament.[65] In addition, people have particular events or situations that always seem to cause intense emotions. We call these events *triggers*.

Whenever <u>my sister plays with my books without permission</u> (trigger), I get very angry.

Triggers are personal, they vary from one person to another and indicate things that are important to that person. At the same time, young people and adults have predictable reactions when they experience certain emotions. These predictable behaviors are called *behavior patterns*.

Whenever I get angry with my sister, <u>I yell at her </u>(pattern).

While many behavior patterns can be helpful—such as consistently putting the homework in the backpack to take home—they can also be hurtful to others and/or get in the way of learning. Can you remember having a student in your classroom who always got in trouble for the same reason? He probably had a clear behavior pattern but did not realize it, or he was unable to see any other way to deal with a situation.

Behavior patterns tend to be automatic—we do them without really thinking, they are part of who we are—which makes them harder to change. However, when students start to identify those typical reactions that are not that helpful, they realize they have *alternative choices* when it comes to their behavior. They don't have to react in that particular way; they can use a calming strategy first, and then choose a different course of action.

When I get angry with my sister, <u>I will walk away</u> from the situation. Once I am calm, <u>I will talk to her</u> about not playing with my books.

Although this change might not happen right away, being able to identify those behavior patterns can be a powerful process for students, like turning on the light in a dark room. It requires students to observe themselves "from the outside," as if they were the main characters in a movie.

Teaching students to identify triggers and behavior patterns is an important part of building their self-awareness and increasing their capacity to return to the green zone so they can make better decisions. With time, most children learn how to be more responsive and less reactive when faced with difficult or triggering situations. Check out the Direct Instruction section, on page 108, for specific ideas on how to support your students in identifying triggers and behavior patterns.

3. **Reframing with optimism**

Ms. D's second grade students are working independently, creating graphs of trash items collected during a recent visit to the local beach. Mariana is writing on a white board, listing the number of items she collected: four plastic bottles, 10 plastic utensils, one broken cooler. She is about to start graphing these numbers in her notebook when Ms. D calls to the class, "One more minute, Beavers! Please finish up your graphs so we can count all the trash items the class collected."

Mariana goes back to her notebook. She wants to use a pie chart to show her results. She divides the pie into 4 parts for the plastic bottles, then she starts dividing the pie into 10 parts, but stops and looks at the chart confused. "This doesn't make any sense! This is stupid." Frustrated, she throws her notebook away. Ms. D approaches Mariana and asks her what happened. "I'm not good at math. I'll never learn how to graph things, especially stinky trash. This is a horrible classroom!" Mariana responds and walks away. Does this situation sound familiar?

Students, and adults too, create explanations for the things that happen in their daily lives. In this situation, when Mariana gets frustrated and gives up on the task, she explains the cause of this situation in a pessimistic way. She blames herself ("I'm not good at math"), believes that the event will persist forever ("I'll never learn how to graph things"), and generalizes this situation to her overall experience in that class ("This is a horrible classroom").

Pessimism and Optimism

Although such explanations may seem harmless, researcher Dr. Martin Seligman has found that people who explain their experiences in pessimistic ways have a higher risk for depression, lower academic and professional achievement, and lower-quality physical health than those who hold optimistic views.[66] The good news, according to Seligman, is that we are not born pessimistic or optimistic—these are ways of thinking that we learn from our families and teachers, the media, and our social context. Think about a recent event in your life, either good or bad—what did you tell yourself about the causes of the event? Were they more pessimistic or optimistic?

Pessimistic explanations include the ideas that causes are permanent, pervasive, and personal, while optimistic explanations are that causes are temporary, specific, and changeable with effort. Look at the chart below to see how Mariana could have reframed the situation using an optimistic perspective.

As educators, we cannot always anticipate when students will face stressful events in their lives, but we can work to provide them with the necessary skills to navigate successfully through life. Being able to reframe challenging situations with optimism is an important aspect of Elect Our Responses—the second HEART skill—which will help us to respond to small and big challenges.

	The Pessimist	**The Optimist**
Permanence	Permanent: "I will never learn how to graph things."	Temporary: "I was not able to figure out how to do a pie chart today."
Pervasiveness	Universal: "This is a horrible classroom."	Specific: "This activity was frustrating."
Personalization	Internal: "I am not good at math."	Changeable with effort: "If I practice, I can get better."

4. **Finding choices**

Finally, Elect Your Responses includes an active process of exploring the choices and/or alternatives in our everyday decisions. When teachers explicitly teach social and emotional skills in their classrooms, a time comes when students realize, "Wait, that behavior causing me/others pain/trouble is not my only choice. I can do other things with my anger and frustration. That behavior is not me." This is a powerful moment in the development of students' self-management, realizing they have the power to choose their behaviors and reframe the challenges they encounter. As we have discussed before, students and adults are not able to clearly see these choices when they are in a fight-flight-freeze response, and that is why this skill starts with managing emotions.

Once we are in a place of calm and feel in control, we are better able to explore choices before acting or making a decision. At the same time, when we are able to spot our negative self-talk or pessimistic thoughts, we can create some space to explore alternative ways to look at the challenges we face.

When you first introduce the idea of choices in the classroom, you may need to help students come up with their list for commonly difficult situations. You can help students identify the pros and cons of each choice and then decide which one seems more appropriate, given the situation. Over time, students will be able to do this on their own.

Indicators of Mastery

Beginner (kindergarten through second grade)

- Identifies tools to manage strong emotions
- Describes behavior patterns
- Identifies challenges in daily situations

Advanced Beginner (third through fifth grade)

- Uses self-management tools to manage emotions
- Recognizes own typical reactions to daily situations
- Demonstrates reframing skills in challenging situations

Strategic Learner (sixth to eighth grade)

- Demonstrates behavior and emotion management to maintain focus and concentration
- Explains own patterns and things that trigger certain emotions and behaviors
- Analyzes why one achieved or did not achieve a goal

- Uses reframing skills in daily situations

Emerging Expert (ninth through 12th grade)

- Demonstrates capacity to manage behavior and emotions to maintain focus on one's goals

- Anticipates patterns and articulates tools to change unproductive behaviors

- Identifies the role of attitude and self-talk in success

- Applies strategies to cope with a variety of stresses

Practicing Expert (college and beyond)

- Adjusts behavior and emotions in response to changes in the environment or to changes in one's goals

- Uses tools and strategies to transform unproductive patterns

- Generates alternative solutions to problems and sustains optimism

CLASSROOM APPLICATION

Children of all ages need ongoing support to develop the second HEART skill—Elect Your Responses. Adults often need help in this area too. If you have a dedicated time for teaching SEL in your classroom, make sure you go back to these tools time and time again after you introduce them the first time. Many students quickly learn to articulate what they need to do if their emotions grow big, but they have a hard time using the tools when the moment comes. Encourage students to choose one or two strategies that work for them and to celebrate their accomplishments in this area, big or small. Over time, these tools become part of students' personal toolbox and they grow with students' capacity to cope with challenging feelings when they are older.

Elect Your Responses is a skill that can often be integrated with academic content. Take a look at these suggested tools and strategies, and adapt them as needed to support the particular needs of students in your school and classroom.

Direct Instruction

To help you teach Elect Your Responses more effectively, the Direct Instruction section is organized following the key concepts that we have reviewed—managing emotions, identifying triggers and patterns, and reframing with optimism.

Managing Emotions

Teach *"Name It to Tame It."* As we discussed in Honor Your Emotions, the first skill in the HEART model, naming your feelings helps to decrease their intensity. Dr. Daniel J. Siegel calls this strategy "Name It to Tame It." When students (or adults) are experiencing strong emotions, they can engage their left brain by telling the story of what made them upset—or sad, disgusted, or hurt. When they do this, they start making sense of the experience and feel more in control.

With younger kids, teachers may need to ask questions to help a child tell the story of what happened. Sometimes students will need your help—especially if you observed the situation—to sort out the facts from their perceptions of the situation and their feelings. Sometimes you will need to provide feeling words (verbally or using your feelings word wall), until they are able to do it on their own. In any case, let students tell the story from their perspective. Middle school students may need support naming not only the emotions they experience on the surface but also the feelings that may be hidden. If students are not ready to have this conversation just yet, be patient and approach them at a later time.

Using the breath as a calming tool. Paying attention to our breath has a calming effect on our body and mind—our heart rate slows down, our blood pressure decreases, and we are able to override the alarm that went off in our amygdala. When students experience big emotions and feel out of control, they can go back to the green zone by simply using their breath as a self-soothing tool.

Mindful breathing encourages a curious and kind attitude toward oneself, it is simple to learn and it doesn't require any special materials. Paying attention to the breath, even for just two minutes, can give you and your students great relief. Below, are exercises that you can do in your classroom; choose one or two and practice them regularly with your students. The key here is to introduce these tools when students are calm, so they associate these exercises with a positive experience. Once students know the exercises, if they are experiencing strong emotions, you can suggest they use one of them to calm down and return to the green zone.

- **Belly and Heart Breathing.** Have students put one hand on their belly and the other hand close to their hearts. Ask students to take three deep breaths and notice how the belly and chest rise with each inhale. Have students notice what happens when they breath out.

- **Star Breathing.** Have students put one hand out in front of them, with their fingers separated to form a star. Then, have students use the opposite hand to begin tracing along the hand that is fanned out. Tell students to inhale through the nose as they trace the outside of the thumb, then exhale through the mouth as they glide along the inside of the thumb. Students continue tracing and breathing until all fingers have been traced.

- **Tumble Dryer.** Sitting in a cross-legged position, have students point their index fingers toward each other and position them so the left finger is pointing to the right and the right finger is pointing to the left, overlapping a bit in front of the mouth. Have students blow as they spin their fingertips round each other, making a lovely long exhalation and a satisfying swishy sound.

You can use these breathing exercises during your designated SEL instruction time and during transitions. Please note that these are just a few examples. If you are interested in teaching mindfulness, I would suggest taking a course from organizations such as Mindful Schools and starting your own mindfulness practice at home.

Visualizing memories. Another way that you can teach students to manage their emotions is by helping them visualize a time when they experienced pleasant emotions such as happiness, pride, or contentment, or a time when they were able to manage some uncomfortable feelings in a positive way. For example, some students may feel anxious about an upcoming deadline, changing work groups, or going on an overnight fieldtrip. You can help them regulate these emotions by asking them to remember a time when, despite feeling anxious or scared, they were able to manage these feelings and they had a positive outcome.

Help them identify the strategies they used at the time. Ask them if that strategy would help them in the current situation. This process supports students in recognizing their capacity to successfully manage unpleasant emotions; the goal is for students to *remember* that feelings don't need to determine the outcome of the situation if they use tools to manage them. When we help students remember and understand events from the past, we are supporting them to better understand what is happening to them in the present moment.[67]

Teach the zones of regulation. At the beginning of the school year, and after you have developed your students' emotional literacy, introduce the zones of regulation in your classroom. Create a visual that works for your students' grade level (a stoplight for younger students, emojis for older students), and display it in the classroom. Brainstorm with your students the feelings they may experience in each zone and discuss which zone may be more appropriate for everyday school activities: the blue zone may be appropriate for reflective exercises; the yellow zone for creative or group work; the green zone for tasks that require focus and concentration. You can connect this lesson to what you have already taught students about honoring emotions and paying attention to their bodies. Use this visual to help students during transitions and to develop their self-observation skills.

Identifying Triggers and Patterns

Thermometer of emotions. You can use the analogy of a thermometer to help students understand how triggers increase emotions. A good example to start with is anger, since it can be a difficult emotion for students to manage. Begin by drawing a thermometer—or creating one from tagboard—with marks that show intensifying levels of anger: annoyed, irritated, angry, furious.

Share a story about yourself or about someone who becomes increasingly angry. As the character gets angrier, have a volunteer use a red marker or a piece of yarn to show how the "temperature" increases. With each step, have students help you identify the *event* that *triggered* the emotion: "My husband took my car keys this morning and I felt very angry. What caused me to feel so angry today?" Share with students what this emotion was indicating or trying to communicate to you, "It was very important for me to be on time for a meeting." Ask students, "What happens if we don't do anything to reduce our temperature? What does the doctor say if we have a fever?" Then, introduce the idea of *emotion reducers*, this is where you can discuss the self-management skills we have reviewed ("Name It to Tame It," mindful breathing, visualization). As the character uses one or more of these tools, the temperature goes down. Have students create their own thermometers and have them include the emotion reducers they may use in the situation. Thermometers are also effective for measuring other emotions such as fear, anxiety, or happiness.

Becoming a pattern detective. Discuss with your students the existence of *patterns* in different contexts: the natural world (animals and flowers), in art and architecture (tiles, buildings), or in math (fractals, numbers). Explain to students that a pattern repeats in predictable ways. Then, brainstorm behavior patterns that students have: brushing teeth before leaving for school, packing swimsuit and towel for swim class, lining up in the cafeteria to get their lunch. These are things we do without really thinking; our brain knows what to do. Discuss with your students the things they do without paying much attention when they experience certain emotions. Some of the patterns may be productive, some may not.

When I feel_____, I _____.

Give students the assignment to become pattern detectives—they need to come up with one or two of their own behavior patterns. Have them observe a family member; can they observe any patterns?

Once students are familiar with the concept of behavior pattern, you can use this language when helping them manage difficult situations in school. Asking about these patterns can even become part of the behavior reflection sheets that many schools use when students display inappropriate behaviors in school.

I do my best when. A big part of developing students' self-management skills starts with helping them to know themselves better. Have students create a list of three things that support them in doing their best, and three things that hinder their ability to do their best. Then, have students keep track of how often these situations occur—in your classroom, with other teachers, at home—and discuss the results. Then, help students come up with actions they can take to decrease the number of times they are in situations where they cannot do their best. This may be a good time to discuss things they have control over (sitting in front of the classroom if they get distracted, asking the teacher for additional time to finish an assignment) versus those things they may not be able to change (getting a new computer, doing house chores after completing homework).

This activity helps students develop a deeper awareness of themselves and their likes and dislikes. It can also help teachers get to know their students better and how they think about themselves and their potential.

Reframing with Optimism

Creating choices. During your morning meeting, classroom circle, or advisory period, brainstorm with your students the daily challenges or things that are difficult for them. Then, help them come up with different ways to look at those challenges. You can use prompts like these:

- What do you think when you get a bad grade or don't get invited to a friend's party? (Use examples created by your students).

- How do you explain it to yourself? (Help students question their own thinking.)

- Is there another way to look at the situation?

- What would happen if you looked at the situation from this alternative perspective?

Identifying pessimistic explanations. When students create explanations for the events in their lives, they might not recognize whether their views are optimistic or pessimistic. You can help them identify words and language that express pessimism and optimism. For example, discuss with students the common responses to a challenge or difficult situation. Then, use the pessimistic and optimistic explanations discussed earlier (permanent, pervasive, and personal versus temporary, specific, and changeable with effort) to help students differentiate between their pessimistic and optimistic views. Let's review them.

	The Pessimist	**The Optimist**
Permanence	Permanent: this situation is everlasting.	Temporary: this situation is provisional.
Pervasiveness	Universal: this situation impacts all aspects of my life.	Specific: this is a particular situation.
Personalization	Internal: I cannot change this situation.	Changeable with effort: I can change this situation with practice.

Reframing pessimistic explanations with optimistic ones. Once students can identify their own pessimistic explanations, they can learn to reframe them by looking at challenges as temporary, specific, and possible to change with effort. Use common stressful situations for students—finals, trouble with friendships, sport competitions—and ask them to write down optimistic responses to these challenges. What could they tell themselves if they were more optimistic? When students develop more optimistic views of their daily challenges, they're building resilience for the future and creating expectations for positive outcomes in their lives.

Integration with Teaching Practices

Create a calming corner. This is a quiet area of the classroom or school equipped with soft furnishings and soothing materials to help students de-escalate when they are in the red zone (i.e., feeling very upset). The objective is that students will be able to use the calming corner and go back to class activities independently.

Teachers who have created calming corners in their classrooms report that they spend less time dealing with behavior challenges because students are better able to self-monitor.[68] This strategy helps students develop self-awareness—to honor their emotions—since it creates a space for them to connect with their feelings. It also helps students to practice their ability to elect their responses, as they are encouraged to use any of the available tools in the calming corner to manage their emotions before returning to classroom activities. You may be thinking that students will use this space too much, trying to skip or delay doing class work. You may be right. As with any tool that students use independently, when you first introduce it, you will need to make sure students understand the objective and the rules for using the space. Some teachers keep an hourglass in the calming corner; once the time is up, students are encouraged to return to their work.

A calming corner can help adults, too. I worked with a dean of students who set up a calming corner for adults in her office, stocking it with candles, chocolate, toiletries, and other items that her staff enjoyed. Many teachers would stop by during the day, sometimes to say hello and other times to take a little break.

Implementing quiet time. Consider the high levels of stress and stimulation that students experience on a daily basis and the fast pace of many schools' schedules. Students and adults go from one activity to another, sometimes without any time to process these experiences. When this happens, we are compromising students' learning and adults' well-being. Quiet time provides students with a regular, quiet, peaceful, and restful period to meditate, or to do sustained silent reading or free drawing. It helps students de-stress and refocus and prepare their brains for meaningful learning. The idea is for students to relax without noise or interactions, to just enjoy a peaceful activity for a few minutes.

Feedback loops. Provide students with feedback routinely when they practice electing their responses. Describe specifically what you saw them doing: "I noticed that you used the calming corner this morning and were able to join the group afterward." Pay attention to students' negative self-talk and provide feedback when they reframe their thinking or show perseverance. Ask them to describe how that made them feel so they can build memories that connect challenges with positive outcomes. If you want to systematize this feedback, *you can incorporate social and emotional goals as part of students' personal learning plans.* Students can come up with a realistic and measurable goal to increase their ability to elect their responses; for some students this may mean using soothing strategies when they feel upset, for others, reframing their thinking when they feel stuck and they want to give up. Help students keep track of their progress by creating a checklist or modifying the indicators of mastery for Elect Your Responses included in this chapter.

Integration with Academic Content

Multiple choices (mathematics). An important part of developing the Elect Your Responses skill is supporting students as they expand their awareness of choices—there are different ways to view a situation and several strategies to solve a problem. Since the Common Core Standards for mathematics include students using different methods to solve problems, this is a perfect match. As students solve math problems using different approaches, ask them to identify which strategy they use automatically, without thinking. This will most likely be their pattern. If students get stuck solving problems, ask them to share their thinking:

- What do you tell yourself when you are stuck?

- Is there a different way to approach this problem?

- What could you tell yourself to help you tackle this problem with optimism?

This will help reinforce the lessons you taught during the SEL designated time and will help students apply the skills in a real situation. You can create a poster with the strategies we have reviewed in Elect Your Responses and have students track when they use those strategies successfully in math.

Character analysis (language arts and social science). Students can identify how historical figures or characters in a story respond to emotionally-charged situations or challenging problems. Help students differentiate between a reaction (an immediate action triggered by an event, where there is no consideration of the consequences) and a response (a nonthreatening, calm, thought-out action) in the stories you read in the classroom. Ask students to identify the pros and cons of the decisions characters make, and create a different ending to the story.

- What would have happened if the character had used one of the strategies we reviewed in Elect Your Responses?

- How would that affect the other characters and the final outcome?

- What would happen if the characters had an optimistic perspective?

Students' choices (all subjects). A meaningful way to help students develop their ability to elect their responses is by allowing them to make choices. In order for children and youth to make responsible decisions when they are adults, they need opportunities to practice making decisions, big and small. In the classroom, you may allow students to choose how they are going to show what they learned in their lessons. For example, students could choose between creating a poster or having classmates participate in an experiment. They could have choices about completing an assignment independently or in small groups. Students could choose the topics in their writing assignments.

This is an area that may feel uncomfortable for educators—sometimes it is difficult to let go of our sense of control over the academic content and how we teach it. The idea is not to offer endless choices or let students off the hook for challenging work, but to provide meaningful opportunities for students to share their voices and use them for learning purposes. Psychologists Idit Katz and Avi Assor have found that what matters most isn't the kind of choice given to students, but how students *perceive* the choice; when students associate the choice with feelings of autonomy, competence, and relatedness, then having choices will most likely drive beneficial outcomes.[69]

Offering students choices in their learning has two powerful outcomes. With the one, students develop their ability to elect their responses in "real" situations; as they consider their choices, they will have to analyze the pros and cons of each decision and anticipate the results. "Will I be able to focus if I do this activity with my best friend?" With the other, when done intentionally, having a choice can increase students' engagement and involvement in their learning process. Start small and keep increasing students' choices as you begin feeling more comfortable.

Checklist and self-evaluation tools (all subjects). Who doesn't love a good checklist? If you tend to obsess about planning and organization, you may have read *The Checklist Manifesto* by Atul Gawande. He argues that a checklist is a way of organizing that empowers people to put their best knowledge to use, communicate, and get things done. From the SEL perspective, this is a great tool for helping students put their ability to elect their responses into practice. First, the process of *reading* the checklist allows students to review classroom expectations (both academic and social-emotional) without your intervention. Second, in the process of *answering* the checklist, students are able to monitor their behavior and anticipate their likelihood to accomplish individual or group goals. Lastly, the checklist provides students with an opportunity to make a different choice if they are not on the right track.

When students use these kinds of self-evaluation tools on a regular basis, they develop their ability to engage in reflective processes about themselves and their learning, which in turn supports their ability to make informed and responsive decisions.

Tools for Measurement

In the appendix of this book, you will find a table with the indicators of mastery for each HEART skill. This scope and sequence can help you identify areas where your students need additional support. You will also find a self-assessment survey to help you reflect on your own HEART skills.

A—APPLY EMPATHY

Definition

Applying empathy means recognizing and valuing the emotions and perspectives of others, taking action to support them, and nurturing self-compassion.

Apply Empathy—the third skill in the HEART in Mind model—allows us to see and appreciate the humanity in others. It supports our understanding of how other individuals see and experience the world, and it provides us with the tools to support them. In this case, the verb is to *apply*, which indicates a need to bring ourselves into action.

I did my final internship for my teaching credential in a rural town in Nicaragua, volunteering at a local NGO, Los Pipitos, that supported children with disabilities. During my time there, I worked alongside a *promo-*

tora de salud (community health professional), Martha. I learned important lessons about empathy from her.

Martha and I used to walk several hours a day on the dusty trails of Yalagüina, trying to reach the homes where children with disabilities lived. Most of these families could not afford to send their children to a special education school or even to the local public school, therefore, Los Pipitos educated the families so they could support their kids' growth and development at home.   During the many hours we spent walking, Martha and I developed a close friendship. She answered my many questions about Nicaragua's culture, politics, and poverty with patience and care. Martha had an amazing capacity to connect with the families we visited and show love and concern, even when the things we saw and experienced were difficult.

Here are three key lessons I learned about empathy from watching Martha relate to others:

1. **Empathy starts with self-awareness.** Empathy is being able to walk in someone else's shoes, to feel with them. Having a son with cerebral palsy herself, Martha had walked paths similar to the families we visited. Although it was difficult to watch people in pain, Martha connected with her own emotions so she could open her heart to these families.

As teachers and parents, self-awareness helps us to be more present in any given situation. It can be difficult to model empathy for our students or our own children if we are still thinking about work, an argument we had earlier that day, or our endless to-do lists. Once we have been able to check in with ourselves, even if it means connecting with uncomfortable feelings, we'll be in a better position to connect with others.

2. **Empathy heals.** Another important lesson that I learned from my dear friend is that when we are able to show empathy for others, they feel accepted and understood. We often encountered families who were skeptical of the help we could provide or scared that we would take their child away. Martha was able to validate their feelings, whatever they were, opening the door for conversation and connection.

When we show empathy for children, youth, or other adults, and we connect with their feelings, that connection has a healing effect on whatever they are going through. Showing empathy makes the relationships with our children and students deeper and stronger.

3. **Empathy teaches empathy.** I learned the power of empathy by watching Martha connect with people in the community. When she talked and related to others, she did it from the heart. Martha modeled empathy by connecting with people's emotions and by talking about people's behaviors without judgment.

Children learn how to show empathy from their parents and caregivers, so when adults around them show empathy toward others, they are teaching empathy with their actions. Mary Gordon, the founder of Roots of Empathy, says that empathy cannot be taught in traditional ways, it can only be taught experientially.[70] In this chapter, we will review ways in which you can create classroom experiences that model and teach empathy to students.

Is empathy on the decline?

There is scientific research that backs up the notion that Americans are caring less for others. Dr. Sara Konrath from Indiana University found a steep decline in empathy among young people from 1979 to 2009, which, she thinks, is partially due to a rise in mental health problems among young people and increased levels of inequality.[71]

Parenting expert Dr. Michelle Borba argues that empathy is on the decline, at least in part because of an increase in a me-centered culture portrayed through social media.[72] Think about the rapid increase of platforms and apps that allow youth to share information about their lives with the world, and the expectations that youth themselves have about portraying a perfect social media profile.

Social media can allow youth to connect with and care for each other, however in many cases it becomes a competitive sport for showing how great their lives are. Although their lives may indeed be great, that is generally not the whole story, leaving young people feeling disconnected, lonely, and stressed. According to Borba, this focus on the individual, accompanied by an increase in academic pressure and a decrease in the overall mental health of our youth, creates an *empathy gap*.

This challenge is not only affecting students—adults are also struggling to figure out how to incorporate empathy in the workplace. The 2019

State of Workplace Empathy Study from Businessolver reports that leaders agree with their employees on the need for empathy in the workplace, but critical gaps remain between intentions and implementation.[73] While CEOs understand the value of empathy, they don't demonstrate the skills required for exhibiting empathy; in this survey, 58 percent of CEOs say they struggle with consistently exhibiting empathy in the workplace. Meanwhile, 72 percent of employees would consider leaving their job for a more empathetic organization.

At the core, employees want their employer to empathize with their everyday working lives and respect the need for balance and flexibility, which many employers do not consider. These employees, who might suffer from a negative workplace environment, may be your students' parents; they will also need to be the recipients of empathy, so they can model and nurture empathy in their children. ***Many people, adults included, have a difficult time showing empathy, because it means going to a painful place within themselves.*** Part of showing empathy is being able to manage the anxiety or fear that the feelings of others generate in ourselves and to grow to accept them.

Key Concepts

In order to apply empathy in our daily lives and teach empathy to our students, psychologist and emotions expert Dr. Paul Ekman recommends exploring three different ways to sense another person's feelings.[74]

- **Perspective Taking** refers to our ability to understand another person's point of view—their feelings, thoughts, needs, and actions. This is what Borba calls the "gateway to empathy" because it allows students to understand the world from another person's perspective. Sometimes it is called *cognitive empathy*; you can imagine how the other person feels and what they might be thinking in a difficult situation. This skill helps students and adults to be better communicators and negotiators, it also helps those who try to motivate people. When students and adults develop their perspective-taking skills, they can significantly reduce their unconscious biases: it is easier to have positive interactions with people who look different than us when we are able to see things from another person's perspective. Researchers have found that intervention strategies designed to enhance empathy contribute to reducing bullying behavior.[75]

- **Emotional Empathy** occurs when individuals feel physically and emotionally connected with the other person: "I feel what you feel." They are attuned to another person's inner emotional world, in part, due to the existence of mirror neurons. According to neuroscientist Dr. Marco Iacoboni, mirror neurons are the only brain cells that code the actions of other people. They let us understand the emotions and actions of others by experiencing a milder form of what they experience.[76] For example, when you see someone bleeding, the mirror neurons for bleeding fire up in your brain. This starts activity in your brain that evokes the feelings we typically associate with bleeding. You don't need to *infer* what the other person is feeling, you immediately experience a milder form of those feelings. Iacaboni also found a reduced mirror neuron activity in individuals with autism, which could explain their challenges with social interactions and understanding the emotions of others.

  Emotional empathy is a helpful skill that supports building emotional connections with others. It can also guide students' moral identity—when children and youth are able to connect with the pain and suffering of others, they are more likely to become helpers in difficult situations and less likely to cause pain in others.

  Although emotional empathy has many benefits, it can also lead to burnout when individuals are not able to manage their own emotions. This often happens for those working in helping professions, such as educators or health care providers. If you are feeling overwhelmed by the challenges your students and their parents face, incorporate self-care as part of your teaching principles. In part three of this book, you will find tools and strategies to nurture your well-being. If the feelings persist or you feel burnout, seek professional help in your community.

- **Compassionate Empathy** happens when individuals are moved to take action and help alleviate the distress of others. Helping an elderly person carry groceries to the car, opening the door for a mother pushing a stroller, or volunteering at the local hospital are compassionate acts. Although certain individuals may be more inclined to initially show compassion, research suggests that compassion is contagious. If you are the recipient of compassionate behavior, you are more likely to be compassionate with others. Dr. Dacher Keltner, faculty director of the Greater Good Science Center at UC Berkeley and author of *Born to Be Good*, argues that compassion spreads because giving and sharing feel good: when people feel compassion and they act on it, they feel a sense of shared humanity with people who are in need.[77] Cultivating these feelings of compassion makes people pay closer attention to those who are in need, which in turn encourages individuals to do something about it.

Self-empathy is empathy too

During a workshop about educator self-care, I asked participants to write down on a card what they tell themselves when they make a mistake. Then, I had them exchange cards with the person sitting next to them. One of the participants looked at me nervously and said, "I don't want to give my card to her. I don't want her to feel what I feel when I make a mistake." As you can imagine, we had a very productive conversation about the way we talk to ourselves when things do not go the way we plan or we make an error. In many cases, we cut ourselves down with self-criticism. We may think, "You're an idiot. Why did you do that?" or, "You always make this mistake. Why don't you learn?" Would you ever talk to a friend like that? Probably not. You would try to show compassion and help them see that mistakes are part of being human. You would help them feel better. However, when we are the ones making the mistake, things change—it becomes harder to show empathy toward ourselves.

Kristin Neff, a leading expert on mindful self-compassion, describes it as treating yourself with kindness, the same way you would treat a friend who is having a hard time.[78] It means learning to speak to ourselves like a good friend: "How are you doing? You seem so sad today. Is there anything that I can do to make you feel better?" and then moving ahead to do things that make us feel safe and cared for.

This also applies to children and youth. Many students can become highly critical of their mistakes at a young age, impacting their ability to deal with failure or disappointment. When students learn to develop self-compassion, they can admit their mistakes instead of feeling paralyzed by them (and giving up) or blaming others. Neff's research also shows that self-compassionate people take greater personal responsibility for their actions and are more likely to apologize if they have offended someone.

In many cases, students don't realize they use negative self-talk until educators create the space in the classroom to reflect and have this conversation. For certain students, it can be a powerful experience to realize that treating oneself harshly does not have positive outcomes in the long term. Helping students to nurture self-compassion in themselves prepares them to become more resilient, resourceful, and happy adults.

> *"Self-compassion motivates like a good coach, with kindness, support, and understanding, not harsh criticism."*
>
> —*Kristin Neff*

Indicators of Mastery

Beginner (kindergarten through second grade)

- Describes how others feel based on body and facial expressions

- Recognizes that others may experience different emotions from oneself in similar situations

- Differentiates between positive and negative self-talk

Advanced Beginner (third through fifth grade)

- Describes the expressed feelings and perspectives of others

- Identifies own feelings when others are in difficult situations

- Identifies negative self-talk in everyday situations

Strategic Learner (sixth to eighth grade)

- Predicts others' feelings and perspectives and explains the reasons

- Analyzes how one's behavior may affect others

- Identifies and explains how negative self-talk can impact performance and well-being

Emerging Expert (ninth through 12th grade)

- Analyzes similarities and differences between one's own emotions and perspectives and those of others
- Identifies ways to act with compassion in the community
- Applies strategies to reframe negative self-talk

Practicing Expert (college and beyond)

- Demonstrates understanding of those who have different emotions and perspectives
- Demonstrates ways to act and live with compassion
- Generates strategies to nurture self-compassion in daily life

CLASSROOM APPLICATION

There are many ways to help children develop the ability to apply empathy—role playing, conducting interviews, participating in service learning. As with other HEART skills, it is important that you continuously and intentionally engage students in *applying* the skill, and create a classroom environment that nurtures students caring for each other.

Direct Instruction

Discuss moral dilemmas. Presenting students with situations where there is not a right or wrong answer encourages students to think deeply about the consequences of certain decisions and the implications for the well-being and feelings of others. During your advisory or classroom meeting, present students with provocative questions or tricky situations; have students work in groups to discuss different points of view and come up with solutions. This is also a good opportunity for students to practice their self-management skills—Elect your Responses—and their ability to actively listen and solve conflicts—Reignite Your Relationships—which we will review in more detail in the next section. Depending on the type of moral dilemma you choose, students will mainly be practicing their cognitive empathy.

Role playing. Role playing is a learning structure in which students take the role of a real or imaginary character and act it out. It creates an opportunity for students to take on a different persona (one that may have different values, experiences, or priorities), and connect with the kinds of emotions and thoughts this person would have and the decisions they would make. It can also help students prepare for difficult situations. For example, students can practice what to do if they are being pressured by peers to do something they don't want to do or, alternatively, how to solve a conflict with a sibling. By acting out situations like these, students develop empathy and build up the experience and self-confidence that give them more tools to respond with when these situations happen in real life. To set up a role-playing exercise, follow these five steps:

Step 1: Identify the situation. Use a challenging situation relevant to students' lives; introduce the problem, and discuss the important issues with students. Share with students the expected outcome of the role playing (i.e., come up with a compassionate solution to the situation, make sure all voices are heard, repair harm that's been done). The scenario should have enough details to feel real and credible. Ask students to submit anonymous, challenging situations that they experience.

Step 2: Assign roles. Identify the characters involved in the situation; you can assign them or have students choose. In the scenario, you will probably have some supportive characters and others that are confrontational. Students need to imagine how their character feels, understand their motivations and goals, and then act out accordingly. Those students without a specific role become observers.

Step 3: Act out the scenario. Each student assumes their role and acts out the situation. Students might become more hostile as the role-play takes place. You are the facilitator—if you see a situation becoming out of hand, stop the role playing and do a quick check-in (how are they feeling? What are they thinking? What is their purpose?) Once the check-in is done, you may remind students of the expected outcome. Some may need to step up, while others may need to show more flexibility. Then, encourage students to continue until they reach the goal or the time is up.

Step 4: Debrief the role playing. Reflecting on the exercise is an essential part of this activity. During the debrief, ask the "actors" what they learned from their character and how it felt to play the role. Help them identify the ways in which characters showed care and compassion and the ways they didn't. How did the students gain perspective about other people? Students playing the role of observers can also share their experience during the role playing.

Step 5: Connect the role playing to real life. Ask your students to reflect on how this situation might play out in real life. What did students learn that they can apply in similar situations in the future? What actions would they try to avoid? Help students connect their learning to their own lives.

Examples:

Situation 1: Your two best friends are making fun of a new student in your class. She just arrived from another country and does not speak much English. You also came from another country and know what if feels like to be the new kid. You try to stop your friends from making fun of this student.

Roles: two teasing students, new student from another country, student who tries to stop the teasing

Situation 2: Your friend is telling you about having to put his dog to sleep. He is very upset and starts crying. You have never seen your friend cry before and do not know what to do. As he is telling you the story, two other students walk by and say, "Oh, look at the crybaby! Do you need your pacifier?"

Roles: student who owns the dog, student who is listening to his friend, two teasing students walking by

Situation 3: Your school's coach is organizing a sporting event to celebrate the end of the school year. Although "all are welcome," it bothers you when you see that all the activities require students to be strong athletes. Some of your classmates agree with you, others don't see your point. You have a conversation with the coach about it.

Roles: coach, students questioning the event, students in favor of the event

Discovering negative self-talk. During your morning meeting or advisory period, share with your students a recent situation where you made a mistake and how you felt. On a flip chart, write the negative things you told yourself when you discovered your error. Discuss with your students how these thoughts impacted your feelings and the things that you did afterward. Invite one or two students to share a mistake they recently made, write down their negative self-talk and discuss the consequences. With your students, come up with alternative thoughts you can have when you make a mistake. Invite students to create a poster for the class with positive statements that encourage students when they make errors, are feeling stuck, or are overwhelmed by a situation.

During the day, regularly check in with students about their thinking—what are you telling yourself about this challenging equation? What is your brain telling you about feeling left out by your friends? Then encourage students to use some of the positive statements the class has generated. The goal is for students to develop awareness of when they are having negative thoughts and intentionally replacing them with other more encouraging and supportive thoughts.

Integration with Teaching Practices

Monitoring caring moments. Students pay attention to those things that we educators emphasize on a daily basis. Ms. B., a first grade teacher in Memphis, Tennessee, has a visual display of the caring moments that she and her students observe in her classroom. Every time they observe a caring moment—it could be a student helping or comforting another student after a frustrating situation, or someone doing something extra to take care of the classroom—they write down the situation on a Post-it Note and graph it. Once every few weeks, the class spends some time reading these notes and summarizing the data collected. They discuss the feelings of the students involved and what moved them to show compassion. They also analyze how the data has changed over time—is the class increasing or decreasing the number of caring moments?—and the possible reasons.

Encouraging redos. Human beings are not perfect, we make mistakes all the time. We often make mistakes because of an impulsive decision, lack of information, or because we simply did not know what else to do. Other times, we don't stop to think about how our actions could affect others. Encouraging redos in the classroom teaches students that mistakes are part of being human and that there is an opportunity to try again. This is an important part of establishing strong and positive relationships as we will see in the following HEART skill. Encouraging redos can also be applied in academic situations, such as when students do not get the grade they expected or they're missing some parts of a group project. By allowing students opportunities to "try again," we are teaching the value of effort versus a sole focus on outcome.

Learning buddies. Children and youth can also develop their empathy by becoming learning buddies for younger students or students in their class. Learning buddies function like reading buddies, but instead of focusing solely on reading, they provide academic and social and emotional support for other students. If you organize learning buddies in the classroom, you can pair students with shared interests, academic skills, and personal choices. The idea is that students will be able to check in with each other during the day to see if their buddy needs any help with completing an assignment, getting their desk organized, or choosing a book from the library. A buddy might also help a fellow student solve a conflict with a peer or get over an argument with a sibling. Learning buddies can become part of the way students support and help each other in your classroom, allowing you to focus on the things that only you can do. When students help each other on a regular basis, they apply their empathy and create a climate of care and kindness in the classroom.

Service learning. Community or school-based service activities are among the most effective resources for helping students develop empathy. When students are actively involved in activities that benefit other students or the community, they develop a better understanding of other living things—people, animals, or plants—and the problems that affect their livelihood. Service learning projects are generally connected to classroom instruction and specific academic standards, so students develop their academic skills along with social and emotional competencies. Service learning includes time for reflection on what happened during the experience and as a result of it; this is a perfect time to help students reflect on their HEART skills and on their ability to connect with others and share their feelings.

Integration with Academic Content

How would I feel in this situation? (language arts, social studies). Language arts and social science lessons offer great opportunities to help students develop their ability to recognize what other people feel and experience. When you read books in class and study historical or current figures, spend some time exploring how students would feel in different situations, and have them describe that person's point of view. For example, you may ask students to imagine they are Rosa Parks, the American civil rights activist who refused to relinquish her seat in the "colored section" of a Montgomery, Alabama, bus to a White passenger. Ask students to use the first person, so they can connect with the feelings that Rosa may have felt:

> I am Rosa Parks. I feel embarrassed and saddened by the way African-Americans are treated in this country. I am scared, but I also feel brave to stand up for my people.

By using the first person, students can more easily put themselves in the situation and be sensitive to the emotions and experiences of others. It is also an opportunity to discuss how most people can experience several emotions at the same time. If you do this on a regular basis, when analyzing characters in novels or studying historical figures, you will be building students' habits of imagining and connecting with how others feel.

Interviewing people to develop complex characters (writing). In a way, empathy is about being curious about other people, their experiences, and ways of life. Conducting interviews is a great way to fulfill our curiosity, hearing about people's everyday lives, their needs, and the challenges they encounter. As you work with your students in developing their writing, use interviewing as a tool to help them gather important information about people's lives, so they can create complex characters in their writing while developing their empathy.

If you work with younger students, they may interview family members or neighbors. If you work with older students, you might ask them to interview members of the broader community. If you have technology resources in the classroom, consider using them to connect your students with children from other areas of the world, so they can learn from each other and develop their capacity to see things from different perspectives.

Identifying people's perspectives during current or historical events (science and social studies). When you are exploring current or historical events with your students, identify the major groups involved in the event (i.e., the North and the South during the American Civil War). Ask students to respond to a writing prompt as someone who belonged in one of the identified groups. For example:

> Describe your life as if you belonged to that group: where you live, the type of work you do, your family and friends, your values and beliefs, your needs, challenges, and overall feelings.

Pair up students from the different groups and invite them to discuss their different perspectives. After each partner shares, the other partner must paraphrase what they heard. Once the students are done, come back as a class and reflect on the experience. You can use these prompts to guide the conversation:

> What did you discover about your partner's perspective?
>
> Did you identify any similarities and/or differences?
>
> What does this activity teach about empathy and perspective taking?

Tools for Measurement

In the appendix of this book, you will find a table with the Indicators of Mastery for each HEART skill. This scope and sequence can help you identify areas where your students need additional support. You will also find a self-assessment survey to help you reflect on your own HEART skills.

R—REIGNITE YOUR RELATIONSHIPS

Definition

Reigniting your relationships means nurturing a positive and supportive network by actively using communication and conflict resolution skills, and by working cooperatively with diverse individuals and groups.

There is one year in my teaching career that I remember with acute nostalgia. It was a time when I clearly felt the magic of meaningful relationships. I was new to the school and was called there to take the place of a well-loved teacher who was on sick leave. The students did not want me there. They missed their former teacher and were counting the days until he returned. As things sometimes go, this teacher was not able to return to work, and I stayed. My partner teacher, Toni, had been at the school for more than 15 years. He was warm and funny and cared deeply about the children. We quickly connected and had a lot of fun working together. Although he had a lot more teaching experience than I did, he was generally open to my suggestions and ideas for new projects. He made me feel welcome and part of the team; he was there when I needed support with my class or just to vent about students' behaviors. With his support, I was able to earn my students' trust and we ended up having a great year.

If you have had a similar experience in your teaching career, you know how important it is to have supportive and caring colleagues. Not only are these relationships important for teachers' well-being but they also influence how teachers feel about their teaching and the relationships they establish with their students. Let me explain why.

The way we practice our social and emotional skills is influenced by context.[79] For example, if I had a partner who complained and gossiped about other teachers, or who ignored me, I would have displayed more negative behaviors. On the other hand, when people work in supportive and welcoming environments, they are more inclined to successfully manage job stressors (such as handling a challenging class) and to ask for or offer help when needed.

Now, think about your current workplace. How does it affect your behavior and the ways in which you relate to students, colleagues, and families? Are you able to be your "better self?" Being aware of how your work environment affects your behavior will help you make different choices if necessary. Whenever possible, surround yourself with supportive colleagues. While you may have less control over certain aspects of your school's climate, you play a big role in creating an environment in your classroom that is conducive to positive relationships, enjoyable experiences, and meaningful learning. A big part of this endeavor is developing students' relationship-building skills, so they can learn how to work with different people, have productive disagreements, and know how to "find their place" in a group.

As you have probably experienced in your professional and personal life, for relationships to be strong and long-lasting, you need to cultivate them. In a way, relationships are like a fire—sometimes you have to build them from scratch, using tinder and kindling, while other times you can sit back and enjoy the warmth before adding more fuel. This is why the verb in this competency is *to reignite*, which means to burn again, to give new life and energy.

Although relationships are an important part of children's healthy growth and development, they are often difficult to navigate.

- An embarrassing picture was posted on social media, and now she does not want to go back to school.

- He decided to play tag instead of soccer during recess, and his friends stopped talking to him.

- They lost the school's rope competition, and now the other students make fun of them in the cafeteria.

It is not uncommon for children to feel isolated, rejected, ashamed, or lonely; these are difficult feelings to manage. Being able to honor these emotions—naming them and understanding why they are there—is an important part of the equation, but it is not the only one. Students need tools to navigate their daily environments with compassion and confidence. Let's take a look.

Key Concepts

Reignite Your Relationships entails being able to do the following:

1. ***Using communication to interact effectively with others.*** Being able to effectively express thoughts and ideas, orally or in writing, is a fundamental skill not only in the elementary classroom but also in the C-suite. Communication is key for career advancement and becoming a trustworthy leader in any sector. Adults who can communicate effectively tend to experience better productivity and improved relationships. The thing is that poor communication creates tense relationships and a negative en-

vironment. On the other hand, environments with positive and dynamic communication tend to create the appropriate conditions for learning and high performance.

Although communication skills are learnable and can be developed over time, many students reach college without a clear roadmap of how these skills can be used to create positive outcomes in their academic and personal lives. There are many ways to help students practice their communication skills in the school environment:

- First graders presenting a personal learning project to their classmates.

- Fifth graders writing a letter to the mayor asking for bike lanes.

- Seventh graders holding a Socratic circle.

- High school students creating opinion pieces about current events.

The possibilities are endless! Now, make a mental list of the current activities in your classroom during which students have to use their communication skills orally and in writing. What do you notice? You probably listed most of their daily activities in school. Communication skills are necessary for learning and building positive relationships with others, that is why it is crucial that we support our students in developing these competencies.

The type of communication skills we use depends on the context. For example, we use different strategies depending on whether we are trying to inspire, convince, support, or inform; and we use different formats to meet our goal (small group conversation, email exchange, presentation to an audience, social media campaign). Students will benefit from learning which strategies are relevant and appropriate for each situation, so they are able to communicate with their audience more effectively.

Voice 21 is a campaign to raise the status of oracy—the ability to articulate ideas and communicate with others—in schools across the United Kingdom. Although their focus is mainly on oral language, they have developed a framework that I find useful in understanding key aspects of communication. They set up four strands that enable successful discussion and effective communication—physical, linguistic, social-emotional, and cognitive. I use these four strands to explore how you can support your students' communication skills from a social and emotional perspective.

Physical. Brian is trying to get his classmates to agree with his proposed project; he is frowning with crossed arms and elevates his voice when someone disagrees. His voice and body language seem to indicate frustration and perhaps some resistance to hearing others' opinions. Since emotions are contagious (see page 24 for a review on this), Brian's classmates will likely react to his body language with frustration and resistance. Although Brian's intention was persuasion, his nonverbal communication was sending a different message. This happens to adults too! If you are not aware of it, it can hinder your ability to become an effective communicator and meet your goals.

We share information about our thoughts, feelings, and needs through our voice and body language. Paying attention to this nonverbal communication is important for understanding the messages we send to others and changing the way we use our voice and body if it is not helping us to reach our audience. Students can learn how to project their voice, use clarity of pronunciation, and slow down if their speaking pace is too fast. They can practice using their tone of voice to convey different emotions. For body language, students can explore posture, facial expression, and eye contact when doing presentations or working in groups. Videotaping students and having them watch themselves can be a powerful tool. For more details on how to do this, see the Direct Instruction section on page XX.

Linguistic. This is where language lovers go to town. The use of metaphors, humor, and irony are all tools that students can learn and develop to become better communicators. In many countries, these elements are mandatory in the language curriculum, which means teachers are already teaching them in their classrooms. In the context of establishing positive relationships, this is an important area to consider because words are powerful tools. They can be used to hurt, shame, or enrage; they can also support, soothe, and calm someone who is suffering. Words can help people connect at a human level or increase division and hate. They can have a positive or negative impact on other people's lives, as well as on our own. We cannot treat words lightly.

In addition, language is not neutral—it is connected to our identity and culture—and can be unintentionally used to diminish the contributions of our BIPOC students. Supporting our students' linguistic skills requires that we invite students to bring their identities and styles of expression into the classroom, and "support students' academic language acquisition by drawing upon their informal language use."[80]Dr. Christopher Emdin, author of *For White Folks who Teach in the Hood . . . and the Rest of Y'all Too* and professor at Columbia University Teachers College, recommends that teachers use code switching—alternating or mixed use of two or more languages, especially within the same discourse—to support students in valuing their own culture while appreciating and understanding the codes of other cultures. [81]

Social and emotional: listening, awareness, and confidence. We know that listening skills are important for effective communication and also for establishing positive relationships with others. Unfortunately, listening is not a top priority in today's world. In his 2013 book *Focus*, Daniel Goleman observed that poor listening has become endemic. The increased pace of work and life in general, and the never-ending lists of texts and emails that demand our attention impoverish our ability to pay attention and fully listen.

We tend to think of attention as a switch that's on or off—we're focused or we're distracted. According to Goleman, that's a misperception. Attention comes in many varieties, and its extreme forms tend to be the most limiting. When we're too attentive, we fall victim to tunnel vision; the mind narrows. When attention is absent, we lose control of our thoughts: we turn into scatterbrains. Goleman explains that *open awareness* lies in a particularly fertile area between those two poles.[82] Have you observed these two extreme forms of attention in yourself and your students? When are you and your students better able to pay attention?

Dorothe Bach from The Center for Teaching Excellence defines radical listening as, "Listening with the intention to be a vessel for your partner, to be a sympathetic witness so that unspoken meaning may have room to find words. Radical *listening* encourages both speaker and listener to reside in the moment, non-judgmentally."[83]

During your next conversation with a student, a colleague, or a relative, try to follow these listening instructions:

- Quiet your mind and heart.
- Hold space for the speaker.

- Express your attentiveness nonverbally (using facial expression, body language).

- Note the speaker's nonverbal communication.

- Use silence.

- Refrain from making comments, interpretations, or suggestions.

- If appropriate, reflect back the words of the speaker.

Poor listening is becoming the norm rather than the exception, but it doesn't need to stay that way. Listening is an acquired skill, something students can develop over time with practice. Invite students to adapt and modify these tips for radical listening in your classroom, so you can have a common language for observing and practicing effective listening.

In addition to strengthening their listening capacity, students also need to develop their confidence: the belief that they can speak in front of an audience or make a new friend at summer camp. In my own experience, practice is the best ally when it comes to developing a sense of self-assurance when speaking or writing. Providing opportunities for children and youth to try out public speaking in a low-stakes environment—receiving feedback, implementing changes, and trying again—will build their confidence. Similarly, confidence comes from supporting students in choosing topics of their interest and engaging their purpose so they are more motivated to grow their communication skills in ways that honor their identity and cultural values.

And finally, effective communicators can *read* their audience. When developing this awareness, students learn how to check the audience's level of understanding, read the nonverbal language, and pay attention to emotions and the impact their words have on the audience. With all this information, students can then adjust their actions and guide the interaction to meet their goals. This is difficult stuff! I know many adults who *really* struggle with this. However, we must help children and youth develop these skills—the more opportunities they have to practice these skills in a safe environment, the better prepared they will be to navigate a complex and diverse world. At the end of this chapter, you will find several tools and strategies to get you started.

Cognitive. In my daughter's second grade classroom, students often have small group discussions about the books they read. Some of these conversations can get heated, as students have different opinions about favorite characters or preferred topics. The teacher created some handouts with sentence stems, which helped students provide their opinions without hurting feelings or being rude. These are some examples:

I'm going to have to respectfully disagree with_____, because on this page _____.

I see what you are saying, but I wonder if _____.

I have another way of looking at this _____.

Could I suggest a different idea?

Initially, the teacher had to model and remind students to use these sentence starters. But over time, students started to use them without prompting, not only during literary circles but also in other situations. When students get used to using these sentences, they become very eloquent.

One afternoon, I was telling my daughter how we were not able to go to the beach that weekend because we had errands and chores to do. She looked at me, dead serious, and said, "Mama, I see what you are saying, and I have some ideas for how we can make it happen. What if . . . ?" Then, she proceeded to explain how I *always* focused on the boring stuff, instead of doing fun things. She had a system for doing both. Well, I had to smile . . . but also became anxious imagining her as a teenager!

Students' ability to have productive disagreements is an important piece of being an effective communicator, but it does not end there. It allows students to advocate for the things they need and want, not only in school but also out in the world.

2. ***Preventing and solving conflicts in constructive ways.*** It is hard to imagine a healthy relationship that is free of conflict. Conflicts are normal: they are part of living, sharing, working, and interacting with other human beings. They generally emerge when there is a disagreement about ideas, feelings, or needs between people or groups. Too often, we don't solve simple conflicts or process the emotions that come from them. Children and youth may act out their emotions in the form of

physical aggression, gossiping, teasing, or alienating the other person or group.

When she was in second grade, my daughter decided to write a story about dogs with Elena, one of her classmates. They created a Google document and both worked on the story separately and on their own time. One morning, my daughter opened the document and saw that her friend had deleted most of the sentences she had written the day before. She got very upset and emailed Elena *demanding* that her sentences be put back in the story. The girls exchanged a few hurtful emails, until the parents realized what was going on. Elena didn't like where the story was going and had decided to create a different story on her own. My daughter felt mad and heartbroken for days; she had a hard time believing that her friend wouldn't like her work. Elena's feelings were also hurt; she felt disappointed that the story didn't turn out the way she wanted and that her friend wouldn't go along with her ideas.

In this case, the two girls reacted to their difficult emotions by writing hurtful things to each other. They didn't solve the issue, and they remained distant for months after the incident. When conflicts go unsolved, they may impact the quality of human relationships, the climate in the classroom, and students' ability to focus and learn.

Students need to learn how to handle confrontation and develop their problem-solving skills so they can solve conflicts constructively, and educators need to teach these skills within the sociopolitical contexts that impact children's lives, especially BIPOC students. That is to say, educators cannot ignore the conflicts that young people face due to racism, gun violence, homophobia, sexism, and other forms of injustice. Conflict resolution skills should support students—and teachers—to challenge these injustices peacefully, and "become the changemakers and leaders we need."[84]

Learning to solve conflicts involves:

- Effectively expressing our points of view, emotions, and needs

- Actively listening to the other person's points of view, emotions, and needs

- Coming up with acceptable solutions for both parties

- Committing to the best solution

- Executing the plan

Even when we know that conflicts are a great opportunity for learning and development, it is not always evident how to go about solving them! That is why it's important to adopt a conflict resolution process that students and adults can use to solve issues in positive and constructive ways. You can use the HEART skills to help your students reflect on the situation before they attempt to resolve the issue.

H	Honor Your Emotions	How did you feel about this situation in the moment? How do you feel now?
E	Elect Your Responses	What choices did you make? What did you do? Did the problem become smaller or bigger?
A	Apply Empathy	How do you think the other person feels? Why do you think they feel that way?
R	Reignite Your Relationships	Did you communicate your needs to the other person? If you didn't, how can you tell them your needs? Were you able to listen to the other person's needs?
T	Transform with Purpose	What do you want in this situation? What does the other person want? What is your shared purpose in this situation?

Teachers who teach conflict resolution protocols in their schools notice that students become more autonomous and less dependent on adults' facilitation skills.[85] Students can solve issues independently, which frees up time for teachers to do other important tasks.

3. *Working cooperatively with diverse individuals and groups.* When I was working toward my teaching credential, there was not a single course that did not require students to do group projects. It was a working-in-teams marathon! Once I had made a few friends, I found myself always teaming up with the same people—we got along, knew each other's strengths and weaknesses, and had similar working styles. Overall, we trusted each other

and enjoyed working together. I would dream of getting all these great human beings working together in the same school. Well, that never happened, and my dream crumbled quickly when I got my first teaching assignment.

Young and naive, I arrived at school with high spirits, excited to finally apply what I had learned in college. After several weeks, I realized that none of the experienced teachers had any interest in collaborating, let alone supporting my struggles. I was on my own. I felt very isolated and disappointed with these working conditions—I had expected an energetic group of teachers who planned together and supported each other. Instead, I found individuals who preferred to stay in their classrooms and avoid contact with new teachers. That was a hard year.

Luckily, two years later I was assigned to a school with a different working culture. Although teachers had individual teaching styles, they generally got along and were able to work through disagreements. Mainly, they saw each other as teammates working together toward a common goal. In this environment, I felt a huge relief; it was possible to find a school with a collaborative climate, and I was part of it!

As with many other social and emotional skills, you probably learned how to collaborate with others through practice and a trial-and-error methodology. In my case, it has required paying closer attention to the team's individual strengths, and people's backgrounds and experiences, instead of being focused solely on the end goal. As a "get things done" kind of person, I used to prioritize efficiency over involving others or learning about their different perspectives. As a result, I lost people along the way and then felt frustrated because I ended up doing all the work. Can you relate?

Over time, I realized that I needed to adjust my interactions and contributions to the work—I needed to examine how my privilege and position impacted the dynamics in my team. Sometimes it was appropriate for me to drive the group to focus on the end goal, but at other times it was necessary for me to step aside and let others take the lead. I had to learn from my mistakes in working with others, and I hope that we can better prepare our students to lead and contribute to teams with joy, confidence, and care. In the following table, you will find a roadmap to guide the implementation of collaborative work in the classroom.

A roadmap for collaborative work in the classroom	
Start with your own purpose.	Why do you want students to collaborate in the classroom? What are some of the skills you hope they develop? In your classroom, what does positive and effective collaboration look like?
Create a short list of projects and/ or assignments during which you will focus on deepening your students' collaboration skills.	You can choose longer assignments (such as a project-based learning unit), or a shorter one (such as solving math problems in a small group). This is a way to avoid feeling paralyzed by the long list of activities that require teamwork. In this case, you are selecting a few to get you started.
Assess your students' collaboration skills.	Look at the scope and sequence for Reignite Your Relationships in the HEART in Mind model. Are there any areas where your students need additional instruction and/or supports? With your end goal in mind, and your short list of projects in hand, decide if there are any skills that should be scaffolded. Some of the skills may be related to things we have discussed in this chapter, such as active listening, effective communication, or using a conflict resolution protocol. Others may be related to the other competencies in the HEART in Mind model: Are students noticing their emotions if they get frustrated? (Honor Your Emotions); are they considering pros and cons before making a decision? (Elect Your Responses); are they seeing that others may think or feel differently? (Apply Empathy).
Make a plan for scaffolding and/or teaching these skills before students start working in groups.	This may be a time when you review some of the HEART activities you have already covered with students. Alternatively, you might introduce new lessons that specifically target what we have discussed about communication and conflict resolution in this chapter.
Assign team roles.	Have students practice all of the team roles—you will find details to set this up in the Integration with Teaching Practices section—and discuss the experience with them. Are there any roles that were easier or harder to play? Why? What are some of the specific skills involved in each role? Then, have students try working in teams without roles. What do they notice about themselves or others in the group? How did this affect the team's trust and/or ability to reach the goal?

4. *Developing and maintaining constructive relationships.* Reignite Your Relationships is a big, broad skill in the HEART in Mind model. It requires that we practice the first three sets of skills in the model:

- Honoring Your Emotions: connecting with our emotions and recognizing what (or who!) makes us feel secure, frustrated, or scared.

- Electing Your Responses: looking at our choices and how we respond when we are triggered by our emotions.

- Applying Empathy: practicing empathy and applying our ability to understand the perspectives and emotions of others.

Next we come to relationships, where things get messier because relationships involve a certain level of vulnerability and trust in other people. As earlier noted, that can be difficult for many children and adults who have experienced trauma. It may take more time and effort for them and for us to build the necessary trust that requires working collaboratively with others. Cultural competence is an important component in maintaining constructive relationships with diverse individual and groups—by recognizing the limitations of our own culture and learning how rich other cultures are, we can cultivate cultural fluency and effectively negotiate cultural differences in our relationships.[86]

Educators *can* create the conditions for students to feel safe and supported, so students can fully experience the depth and richness of positive relationships with other children and adults. When we work toward developing friendships, we find ways to establish emotional bonds, while bringing our full identities to the relationship. At the same time, when we are able to solve conflicts productively, or give a friend another chance, we apply our empathy and develop resilience.

Indicators of Mastery

Beginner (kindergarten through second grade)

- Communicates needs and wants, takes turns, and pays attention when others are speaking

- Identifies common conflicts with peers and ways to resolve them

- Contributes to group projects

- Understands and appreciates diversity

Advanced Beginner (third through fifth grade)

- Uses active listening skills and disagrees with others in constructive ways

- Describes causes and consequences of conflicts and uses some strategies to resolve them

- Analyzes ways to work in diverse groups effectively

- Identifies differences in the understanding of cultural norms

Strategic Learner (sixth to eighth grade)

- Analyzes the power of one's own words to hurt and/or support others

- Defines unhealthy peer pressure and uses skills to resolve interpersonal conflicts

- Demonstrates social skills when working in groups

- Develops cultural awareness when establishing relationships

Emerging Expert (ninth through 12th grade)

- Analyzes effective communication strategies and uses them based on personal needs and context

- Analyzes how conflict resolution skills contribute to collaborative work and uses them effectively

- Analyzes how power and privilege influence social dynamics

- Evaluates own contributions in groups, as a member and a leader, with a racial lens

Practicing Expert (college and beyond)

- Uses assertive communication to meet needs without negatively impacting others

- Evaluates effectiveness of own conflict resolution skills and plans how to improve them

- Plans, implements, and leads participation in group projects

- Uses cultural competence and humility in building constructive relationships

CLASSROOM APPLICATION

Reigniting your relationships involves communicating effectively, solving problems constructively, working cooperatively with others and maintaining constructive relationships with diverse individuals and groups. The ultimate goal is connecting with others at an emotional level to enjoy trusting relationships based on our shared humanity. Let's look at how you can create these opportunities in your classroom.

Direct Instruction

Teach active listening. Create an opportunity for students to observe what active listening looks like from the outside, and discuss what they see. You could do this by showing a video or doing a demo in the classroom and then creating a poster with students' observations and key takeaways. In your discussion, talk with students about what active listening looks like on the inside—are their thoughts focused on responding to the speaker or understanding the message? Do they notice any emotions in themselves or the speaker? While the things we observe from the outside can be easier for younger students to identify, challenge older students to pay attention to their thoughts while others are talking. What happens if the speaker completely changes the topic or purposefully says something incoherent? Do they notice?

Adopt and teach a conflict resolution protocol. We have discussed the importance of adopting a conflict resolution protocol to give your students a process for confidently preventing or solving conflicts. The key here is consistency. If you introduce the protocol once and never talk about it again, students will most likely not use it. When you introduce the idea of using a protocol, involve students in making it *their* protocol by having them suggest strategies or resources they can use. Check in regularly with students about how helpful it is and modify it as needed. Model using the protocol in conflicts with students or other situations in your life. The more that students can be involved in this process and see a protocol's many applications, the better.

Create discussion guidelines. Discussion guidelines are a helpful way to build classroom community while setting up some ground rules for communication. These guidelines should be created with and by students, rather than being generated solely by the teacher. Guidelines will reflect how the group hopes to interact, share, and communicate. Once you have the guidelines, have students take a quick read before engaging in structured conversations. Point out when you observe students following the guidelines and acknowledge when you fail to follow them yourself.

Community building. The essence of teaching the HEART skills to students is to create community, a place where students have a sense of belonging and want to participate. There is no better way to help students develop their ability to cultivate friendships and strengthen their social skills than by incorporating activities that build community in your classroom. Having a regular classroom circle (sometimes called a morning meeting or council), offers students this opportunity. You can use this time not only to do your explicit SEL instruction but also to provide students a chance to share, offer support, or ask for help. This can be a time when students come together to solve an issue, such as a conflict between peers, and come up with ways to either repair the harm or avoid this situation in the future. You could structure it this way:

- Greeting

- Check-in. How are you feeling today?

- Sharing. This could be open-ended, where students share something they would like the class to know. You can also generate prompts with students; it might be very interesting to learn about the topics they like to discuss. Below are a few examples to get you started:

  o What are you looking forward to this week?

  o What is something new you learned recently?

  o What is something that made you laugh recently?

  o What accomplishment are you most proud of?

  o Can you describe a strength or talent you have?

  o Who is your hero? Why?

  o How can the group help you today/this week?

  o How would you like to contribute to the group today/this week?

- Intention or call to action. This would be a time for students to reflect on something they want to accomplish, a skill they'd like to improve, or a focus they'd like to select for the day. If you have classroom or school values, students may decide to focus on a particular value that day or week.

Students start to open up and share their stories when they feel a sense of trust toward the adults in the room and the other students. No matter what type of classroom meeting you are hosting—one where you are teaching an SEL lesson or one where students are discussing a conflict—your primary role is to facilitate conversation and connection between students. You can share stories or experiences from your own life, but try to avoid making it about yourself. This should be a space for students and by students. In many classroom meetings, students and teachers sit in a circle. The idea of sitting in a circle indicates evenly distributed power and an opportunity for everybody to participate on equal terms.

If you are unsure how to run a classroom circle or how to facilitate this kind of conversation in your classroom, make sure you read Chapter Seven. In that chapter, I discuss how teachers can prepare to teach the HEART in Mind model in their classrooms. It's not hard, it just requires a little practice and a healthy dose of authenticity.

Integration with Teaching Practices

Collaborative structures. Although a certain level of competition can help kids sharpen their skills, it is students' collaboration skills that will support a healthy development and a successful career. When students collaborate, they are united by a common goal and the hostility, fear, or annoyance they may feel toward others will fade away. As much as you can, create opportunities in your classroom where students work together to meet a common goal. These situations help students to know each other better and appreciate the different talents in the group. While individual activities may be easier from a management perspective, students can greatly benefit from experiences where they contribute to a group. These are some examples:

- Group problem-solving. Present students with a problem (one that may have more than one possible resolution) and have them work together to come up with a solution.

- Think-Pair-Share. When you present a question to the group, have students take a minute or two to think about the question. Then, students turn to a partner and discuss their ideas. Finally, students have an opportunity to share the pair discussion with the class.

- Jigsaw. This is one of my favorites. Each student is assigned to two different groups, one is their "home" group and the other one their "expert" group. Each expert group gets assigned a different topic/problem/situation. For example, one expert group topic might be water pollution. Students in that group will research the topic and create a poster to summarize key information. Once they are done, students go back to their home group and teach them about their topic.

Use discussion roles and sentence starters. Discussion roles provide all students with a clear avenue for participation, independent of their HEART skills. When students have a role, they are less likely to feel left out or to disengage, and they are more likely to stay on task. If you rotate the roles within a group, students will have an opportunity to practice different ways of contributing and engaging with the team. They will also be able to experience roles where they feel more confident and others that may be harder or less comfortable. This reflection helps students learn about their strengths and stretch their skills. These are some sample group roles:

- *Team Captain*: makes sure everyone has access to the necessary materials and that everyone is participating.

- *Recorder*: keeps track of the questions and/or agreements within the group. Writes ideas or draws illustrations that show the group's thinking.

- *Time and Goal Keeper*: keeps track of the time and makes sure the team is focused on solving the problem and/or completing the task.

- *Connector*: makes connections between what people in the group think and say. Summarizes key ideas.

Modify these roles depending on your needs, the particular project, and your students' age. Once students have had an opportunity to practice all the roles, you can offer teams a choice of whether they want to have roles or not, then have them reflect on the experience. Building students' understanding of how they learn best it is a natural continuation of this focus on teamwork and relationships.

Sentence starters can help students elaborate their thinking while being respectful toward the comments or opinions of others. Generally, students need the sentence starters early on, but over time, they are able to use conscientious phrasing without reminders. You can find some examples on page 137.

Videotape presentations and collect feedback. Videos are a great way to improve communication skills. If your students do presentations in class, consider recording them so you can look at their communication and presentation skills together. Have students reflect and record "Two Stars and One Wish" for their videos. For example:

Two Stars: what are two things you liked about your performance?

One Wish: what is one thing you would like to improve, change, or do differently next time?

If you record them three times a year, you could review their presentations from the beginning, middle, and end of the school year and reflect on their progress.

Peer mediators and peace helpers. These are students who have been trained to help other students resolve conflicts peacefully; they know the school's conflict resolution protocol well and are able to act as mediators when students have a conflict. They generally work in pairs, with additional support from an adult if needed. When students engage in this type of practice, they become very skilled at solving problems because they have to come up with ways to settle each issue. There is another important lesson here: students learn that they are capable of solving problems *independently*. These are skills that will support students' academic and social-emotional growth.

Integration with Academic Instruction

Philosophical chairs (language arts, social studies, math). This is a great strategy for engaging students in a structured debate about a particular topic. One of the main goals is for students to be open to changing their opinions. First, the teacher or students present a statement for the class to consider. It could be something like, "Buying from local shops is better for the economy than buying from big corporations," or, "Having a shorter recess is better for avoiding conflict between students." First, students spend a few minutes writing down their ideas about the statement and picking a position (yes, no, or undecided). Then, students discuss their positions, providing clear evidence and using some of the communication strategies you have already taught them.

Students are encouraged to pick a different side at any time during the conversation; maybe something someone said sparked some new insights or thoughts about the topic. Finally, students spend a few minutes writing down something that was relevant during the conversation and whether or not they changed their initial position. This is a great exercise to help students develop mental flexibility; it shows that people can change their minds when there are convincing arguments being presented. It is not a sign of weakness to change your mind, it is a sign of growth. For a detailed description of this strategy, you can read college readiness teacher Jill Fletcher's article, "A Framework for Whole-Class Discussions," on *Edutopia*.[87]

Use group evaluation rubrics. When students engage in collaborative projects or any type of group work, it is nice to finish the work by having them discuss their performance based on a rubric. The rubric could incorporate items related to the content of the project as well as the ways in which students used their HEART skills. Here are a few examples:

- Team members felt they were able to contribute to the group project.

- When conflicts arose, the group was able to resolve those issues constructively.

- Team members used eye contact, body language, and a clear voice to communicate with others.

- Everybody felt included during the group work.

You could ask students to complete an individual evaluation rubric first, followed by one completed as a group; that way, you can see the different perspectives within each group. Additionally, students can specify things they would like to do better the next time they work together as a group. This helps build ownership over the project and the use of their HEART skills in academic settings.

Use students' interests, diverse identities, and cultures to enrich academic content. No matter what subject you teach—math, science, language arts, or any other—you can help students develop their relationship skills by creating opportunities for them to share and learn about each other and their personal and social identities.

When students have an opportunity to know each other and learn from their varied experiences and perspectives, they are able to establish stronger bonds. This can be done in the context of academic learning; for example, you can select reading passages that are connected to students' lives—like a story about exclusion in school—and choose books written by authors that represent students' cultures and ethnicity. Too often, students don't want to read their assigned readings because the characters don't look like them; they cannot connect with the stories. By creating a diverse library in your classroom, you can discuss with students not only the content of the book but also why those stories are important.

The opportunities that you create for students to share and learn from each other in your classroom can have a significant impact on the ways in which they interact with academic content and perform in class.

Tools for Measurement

In the appendix of this book, you will find a table with the Indicators of Mastery for each HEART skill. This scope and sequence can help you identify areas where your students need additional support. You will also find a self-assessment survey to help you reflect on your own HEART skills.

T—TRANSFORM WITH PURPOSE

Definition

Transforming with purpose means using personal assets and interests to positively contribute to self and others.

Sixteen-year-old Swedish climate activist Greta Thunberg has become a global icon. In August 2018, she took time off school to demonstrate outside the Swedish parliament, calling for stronger climate-change action. Other students joined her efforts, protesting in their own communities. Together they organized a school climate strike movement, called Fridays for Future. In September 2019, Greta gave a speech to hundreds of thousands of people in New York at the Global Climate Strike. Just a few days later, she spoke at the United Nations and told world leaders, "How dare you? You have stolen my dreams and my childhood." Greta is intrinsically motivated to take action on a topic that worries her. She is moved by a clear sense of purpose and concern for the future and represents a positive role model for youth involvement in important topics.

Sadly, our current educational system is not focused on encouraging students to act on the problems they see in their communities or in cultivating a sense of purpose.[88] Increasingly, the system is focused on individual performance and achievement, with the promise that once students get into college they will be able to engage in activities or topics of their interest. For some students, this may mean *years* of waiting to do something that stirs their imagination. Schools should be places where students' interests and curiosity are engaged and where they can discover their deepest passions and the gifts they can provide to the world. The results of students' disengagement are daunting.

In 2019, internal surveys conducted at a suburban public high school in California determined that 75 percent of their students felt unhealthy levels of stress and anxiety. This high school is not unique. Stress, anxiety, and self-harm rates are on the rise in the US. These things not only impact students' experiences in school but also are indicators of mental health problems in adulthood.[89]

Researchers from the Stanford-based organization Challenge Success have found that 34 percent of middle school students and almost half (49 percent) of high school students work hard in school but rarely enjoy or find value in their schoolwork.[90] These students tend to have higher levels of academic stress (due to grades, quizzes, and tests) than those students who are more engaged in school. At the same time, the American Psychological Association's "Stress in America Survey" (2014) found that school was the main source of stress for teenagers (83 percent), followed by getting into a good college or deciding what to do after high school (69 percent).[91]

We know that schools and teachers can implement changes that address these issues. It starts with believing that students themselves have important ideas about how their schools could better support them. Transform with Purpose, the last skill in the HEART in Mind model, is the place where students' voices are elevated and where educators and students partner to bring about change to improve their communities.

Dr. William Damon, professor of education and purpose researcher at Stanford, defines purpose as a "stable and generalized intention to accomplish something that is at once meaningful to the self and of consequence to the world beyond the self."[92] Damon's definition has two important and related components: First, purpose has to be relevant and significant for the individual. Therefore, it cannot feel like an imposition or something that "needs to be done" to please or make others happy. Second, it needs to contribute to others and the world in some way, beyond the self.

Transform with Purpose echoes Damon's definition and is perhaps the most important competency in the HEART in Mind model. Too often we forget to connect with our "internal compass" (or to teach others to discover their own), and we may find ourselves lost, confused, or thirsty for meaning. Having a sense of purpose has been found to contribute to well-being, especially in the areas of good health and life satisfaction.[93] It helps youth and adults to maintain their motivation and a sense of hope for the future. It is an internal driver to do good in the world.

Having purpose also helps us to use our HEART skills more intentionally. When we have clarity about what to do to move forward in our lives, we are more likely to connect with our emotions, pay attention to the decisions we make, and nurture our empathy and relationships with others. The verb *transform* has a special meaning here—it refers to the fact that a new reality is created—hopefully a better one—when we can act on our purpose.

Cultivating purpose in our students can positively impact their long-term motivation for learning and develop their civic engagement. When students are able to develop a sense of purpose and seek opportunities to act on it, they can become more focused and resilient when faced with challenges.

As with the other competencies in the HEART model, purpose is influenced by life experiences, context, and individual factors.[94] In the United States there is a tendency toward an individualistic approach to purpose development, while other cultures understand purpose from a collectivistic perspective that considers "what is best for the group."[95] These are not right or wrong approaches, but different ways in which cultures influence how we conceptualize and behave in the world. In a way, Transform with Purpose is a way for students to make sense of their personal stories and individual experiences in a particular context, so they can develop personal goals that organize their decisions and contribute to the betterment of their communities. Students' individual trajectories may look very different from each other, but it is possible to support them at each stage of their schooling. In that process, students will benefit and learn from seeing adults at school who are purpose-oriented and who can serve as models for what it means to live a purposeful life.

Key Concepts

Transform with Purpose entails being able to do the following:

1. **Looking inward: What do you care about? What sparks your interest? What's important to you?** These questions have to do with how we practice the first two skills in the HEART model. If we know ourselves and honor our emotions, we will most likely be able to describe our interests and the things that spark our imagination; we can identify what is important to us in our hearts. If we pay attention to our choices and elect our responses consciously, we put

ourselves in the driver's seat and move away from functioning on autopilot. Through this process, we look inward in order to be able to contribute to the world with our interests and values as a guide.

2. **Looking outward: What are some local or global problems you would like to solve?** First, we engage students in exploring and identifying community and global needs based on students' interests and the things they care about. For some students this might be researching animal shelters, for others it may be identifying ways to reduce plastic usage, and, for a third group, perhaps studying their family immigration story. But the work doesn't stop there. Depending on students' race, gender, home language, social class, or sexual orientation, they experience the world in different ways. They may be exposed to microaggressions, discrimination, or homophobia on a regular basis. The second part of looking outward involves analyzing the world with a critical lens so that, with your guidance, students can start to understand why these local and global problems are happening in the first place. While racial, ethnic, and class inequities are often justified by blaming them on a person or a group, we need to analyze and discuss the systemic and structural explanations for differential treatment and outcomes.[96] Students may consider questions such as:

   a. Why is this a problem?

   b. What parties are involved in this problem? What are their perspectives?

   c. Who is benefiting from this problem? Who is being affected by it?

   d. Where do you most often find this problem?

3. **Getting into action: How can you use your interests and talents to positively impact your community and the global needs you care about?** The third step involves aligning the two processes described earlier, looking inward and looking outward. This would be a time for students to reflect on how they can use their interests, talents, and values (identified in the first step) to solve the problems they've identified in their local and global communities.

It is important that students have an opportunity to act on their purpose while in school and to reflect on and share this experience with others. If you are working with younger students, you might facilitate learners getting involved with school improvement projects; as students get older, they can use technology and youth organizations to act on their purpose. There are several additional skills that students will be developing through this process. First, they will recognize a sense of agency about what they are able to do and how their contributions can positively impact others. Second, students will be developing their executive functioning skills so they can design and implement a plan of action successfully.

Although this may all sound overwhelming or even scary, think about it as an iterative process for you and your students. The important thing is that students have a chance to engage in these deep reflections and conversations, so they can develop a sense of purpose and have a place where they can act on it. The final "product" is not as important as the process of searching for purpose, which, hopefully, will be revisited by individuals many times during their lifetime.

Indicators of Mastery

Beginner (kindergarten through second grade)

- Describes personal likes, dislikes, and things that are important

- Identifies assets, problems, and needs at school and in the community

- Identifies steps to address community issues and needs

Advanced Beginner (third through fifth grade)

- Describes personal interests, skills, and values

- Examines community assets and identifies problems and possible solutions

- Performs roles that contribute to improving school or the community

Strategic Learner (sixth to eighth grade)

- Analyzes how personal interests and values influence behavior and outcomes

- Identifies local and global community assets, problems, and their root causes
- Works with community members to address community issues

Emerging Expert (ninth through 12th grade)

- Articulates ways to use personal values, interests, and skills to contribute to others
- Evaluates how systemic problems impact academic, social, and financial outcomes
- Cocreates a plan to address a community issue with community members, using personal strengths

Practicing Expert (college and beyond)

- Applies personal interests, values, and strengths to contribute to others
- Analyzes social, economic, and political structures that maintain inequities and acts to dismantle them
- Monitors progress toward equitable outcomes and living purposefully

CLASSROOM APPLICATION

Direct Instruction

"I admire ____, because____." The goal of this activity and classroom discussion is for students to start thinking about the values they deem important in others and how they can be applied to their own lives. Have students come up with one or two people they admire—an athlete, a scientist, a family member, etc. Then, have students write down the characteristics that make these people admirable. It might be helpful to pair up students and encourage them to discuss the characteristics with a classmate. Did they find any similarities? What about differences? When students have had a chance to share with a buddy, ask the class if they would like to develop these characteristics in themselves, and help students identify what they would need to work on in order to get there. Have students create a paragraph or draw their reflections, and consider displaying the results in the classroom as a reminder of students' commitment.

We are helpers. When students see themselves as helpers, they are more likely to take action and help others in their communities.[97]During your morning meeting or community circle with your students, discuss the positive aspects of their school and the community where they live. Record students' answers on a flip chart. Then, ask students to identify things they would like to change or improve in their school or community, and discuss the root causes of these problems.

This is an important discussion to help students not only to engage in problem solving but also to understand why these things are happening. This is what scholars have called taking a "critical stance" on social, political, and economic issues.[98] Record your students' answers on the same flip chart. Using the students earlier work, defining admirable characteristics and personal values, help students select one or two problems they would like to research further and act on as a class, in small groups, or individually. In this case, you will need to use your judgment regarding the scale of these projects; some of the projects students select may be easy fixes, others may require the involvement of additional adults from outside the school.

Planning for good. Once students have identified one or two things they would like to improve at school or in their communities, they will need to get organized. As a class or in small groups, have students come up with a list of activities that are necessary to get the project started. A good first step might be to gather additional information about the issue by researching on the Internet or interviewing other students or adults on campus. After that, students will need to create a simple plan that describes these activities and who will be doing them. Monitor students' progress to make sure they set up feasible plans and support them with the execution. This may be a positive opportunity to engage families as well. A school-wide yard sale, painting a mural, or creating a garden are a few ways for student to contribute their talents and knowledge outside the classroom in support of a community need.

Milestone Experiences

Students in my local charter school, the San Carlos Charter Learning Center, participate in special, off-campus trips that are unique to their grade level. The trips provide experiential learning opportunities for students tied to the school's core curriculum. As the students get older, these *milestone trips* increase in complexity (and days away from home), challenging students in different ways. For example, students go on a kayaking trip in second grade with one parent, while eighth graders spend four days in San Francisco, navigating the city on their own.

These types of milestone activities are important for children and youth; they mark the end of the academic year with a meaningful experience and offer students an opportunity to use many of the skills they learned during the year. What a great chance for students to practice their HEART skills in a new environment! Researchers have found that field trips effectively support student learning and increase student interest and motivation.[99] Unfortunately, financial limitations force schools to make difficult decisions about how to allocate scarce resources and, in many cases, field trips are not prioritized. If that's the case in your school, there are other things that you can do to create milestone experiences to celebrate students' growth and close the school year on a high note.

Creating milestone experiences

A milestone is a significant event in people's lives and often marks the start of a new chapter. These meaningful events help us grow or change who we are as a person in some significant way. In the school context, milestone experiences should have these ingredients:

1. **Engage the whole child.** It should be an opportunity for students to use, share, and celebrate their unique talents, especially those that they may not use in the classroom. A milestone experience should also provide a space for students to integrate and apply what they know in unique ways.

2. **Challenge students.** The experience should help students move out of their comfort zone and into the stretch zone. Educators

can create a safe space that gently pushes students to go beyond comfort and conformity so meaningful learning can happen.

3. **Build community.** Milestone experiences should offer students an opportunity to connect with their peers and teachers at a deeper level. As we have noted, optimal learning integrates feeling and thinking.

The following are a few examples of milestone experiences that can be done without leaving school.

- **Awards ceremony.** Organize an awards ceremony where every student is honored for something positive, both academic and nonacademic. Students can recognize and celebrate their own work and accomplishments and those of others. This event will help students close the year with a sense of accomplishment and a positive perspective on everything that they were able to do as a learning community. Include families and other educators in this event!

- **School service project.** Have students identify a need at the school, then plan and support students in executing the project. A school-wide yard sale, painting a mural, gardening—there are so many ways for students to contribute their talents and knowledge outside the classroom!

- **Student-teacher unconference.** Teachers and students could plan short lessons on things they are interested in outside of school (music, art, dance, woodwork, crafts). Then create a schedule with instructional sessions for each topic. Students and teachers, maybe even families, can sign up for the sessions they are interested in.

Milestone experiences are a meaningful way to mark the end of the school year, gently pushing students outside their comfort zone and celebrating the learning community that educators create with their students. Milestone celebrations create special memories that you can cherish as you close the year.

Integration with Teaching Practices

Interest-driven learning. When academic content is connected with students' sense of purpose and the things that are important to them, engagement increases. Students are more willing to spend time thinking, discussing with others, and producing quality work when the topics presented in class connect with their interests. While there are certain skills and concepts that teachers need to ensure that students learn, they can also incorporate students' interests into the instruction to make learning more meaningful. For example, students can create models of life cycles using Lego Robotics or they might use soccer data to exemplify equations. If you don't do so already, at the beginning of the school year, consider having students write down the things they like to do outside of school. Then use these topics to:

- Create interest-based writing topics

- Personalize reading materials (this is especially important if you have students reading below grade level)

- Differentiate small group projects

- Provide examples in your direct academic instruction

The key is to connect the content you teach with students' interests, so they become more engaged in class and have opportunities to act on their purpose.

Leadership opportunities. When students have leadership opportunities in their classrooms and schools, they are more likely to act on their purpose and pursue a goal that positively contributes to their schools and communities. In some schools, students organize clubs (i.e., climate change club) that meet during lunch and are open to all students on campus. Schools may consider creating a student committee that helps make decisions about school issues that impact them directly, such as scheduling events and celebrations or student-led conferences. Teachers can get students ready for these leadership opportunities by helping them develop and practice important skills, such as public speaking, active listening, mediation, and decision making. If your school does not currently have any structures allowing students to exercise their leadership skills, you can still create classroom opportunities where students share their voices and perspectives and exercise autonomy.

Student voice and autonomy. In order to help students develop their autonomy, teachers need to relinquish some of the control over classroom protocols, routines, or the content that is taught. While in many cases it is easier (and faster) for teachers to set up the job chart, assign work groups, and select lesson plans, students will not be able to make choices and do things on their own unless they have a chance to practice, make mistakes, learn from these mistakes, and do it again.

In a third grade classroom, the teacher realized that students were not motivated to do any of the classroom jobs she had created for them. To get students to engage and foster their autonomy, she decided to convert the jobs chart into a "needs chart" that was created *with* students. The children came up with the jobs that needed to be done every day and those that needed to be done sporadically, then they volunteered themselves for these jobs based on their skills and interests. Students felt more empowered to contribute to their classroom community and compelled to bring up any needs they saw were not being met through the classroom jobs.

You can foster students' autonomy and engage their voices by allowing them to make decisions about their learning. Here are other examples:

- Provide students with alternative options to complete their assignments.

- Let students choose a topic of interest to develop a classroom project.

- Encourage students to share their opinions through different outlets—letters, newsletters, podcasts, videos, presentations—inside and outside the classroom.

- Organize student-led conferences.

- Encourage students to evaluate their own work and that of others using a rubric.

- Collect feedback from students about your teaching and modify your instruction using this feedback.

Integration with Academic Content

Learning about activists. In keeping up with current events, you can find examples of people who are committed to fighting injustice. Our students should know about the many people who have transformed their lives with purpose in a variety of fields—from science and education to finance and law—and the path that got them there. Teachers can present students with particular individuals as examples and study their values, actions, and the way they may have inspired others to follow their steps.

There are also many examples of youth involved in changing their communities, maybe some of them are in your class! Studying the individuals committed to social justice can be part of your language, mathematics, or social or natural science class, depending on the academic goals that you have for your students. Programs such as Facing History and Ourselves and Teaching Tolerance were designed to integrate social justice and racial, ethnic, gender, and environmental issues into regular academic instruction. These programs can help students and teachers develop their HEART skills and civic responsibility and to act on the injustices they see in their schools and communities.

Critical discussions. Engaging students in critical reflection is an important step toward helping them find a sense of purpose. When students participate in critical discussions, they analyze the root causes of societal inequities, looking for the structural and systemic reasons behind socioeconomic, gendered, and racial/ethnic disparities in education, health, social mobility, and wealth distribution. These discussions can take place in your social science or history classes as many of these issues have a historical context; discussion can help students unpack some of the stereotypes they hold regarding different groups of people in their own classroom or their community. While you may feel vulnerable having these conversations, they can provide students with a safe place to clarify their thinking and have arguments about difficult topics.

Social justice and youth involvement. As we have discussed, building awareness and modeling for students is the first step in developing HEART skills. However, we cannot stop there. Students should be invited to engage in initiatives that build community in their classroom, school, and neighborhood; they should have opportunities to choose their learning and have venues to share their voices. In this process, students and educators work together to create an inclusive and equitable environment where everybody has a sense of belonging and respect. In order for SEL to fulfill its promise, it needs to have an orientation toward purpose, equity, and justice.

Tools for Measurement

In the appendix of this book, you will find a table with the Indicators of Mastery for each HEART skill. This scope and sequence can help you identify areas where your students need additional support. You will also find a self-assessment survey to help you reflect on your own HEART skills.

Endnotes

59   Martínez, Lorea. "Teachers' Voices on Social Emotional Learning: Identifying the condi-tions that make implementation possible." PhD diss., Universitat Autònoma de Barcelona, 2013, http://hdl.handle.net/10803/378029.

60   Ibid

61   Borba, Michelle. *UnSelfie: Why empathetic kids succeed in our all-about-me world.* New York: Simon & Schuster, 2016.

62   "Expressing and Experiencing Emotion." University of Illinois Counselling Center. Accessed September 24, 2020. https://counselingcenter.illinois.edu/brochures/experiencing-and-express-ing-emotion.

63   Dweck, Carol S., and David S. Yeager. "Mindset: A View From Two Eras." *Perspectives on Psychological Science* (February 1, 2019). https://doi.org/10.1177/1745691618804166.

64   Kuypers, Leah. *Zones of Regulation: A Curriculum Designed To Foster Self-Regulation and Emotional Control.* Santa Clara, CA: Think Social Publishing, 2011.

65   Siegel, Daniel J. and Bryson, T.P. *The Yes Brain: How to Cultivate Courage, Curiosity, and Resilience in Your Child.* New York: Bantam, 2019.

66   Siegel, Daniel J. *The Whole-Brain Child: 12 Revolutionary Strategies to Nurture Your Child's Developing Mind.* New York: Bantam, 2012.

67   Katz, Idit, and Avi Assor. "When Choice motivates and When It Does Not." *Educational Psychology Review* 19, no. 4 (December 2007): 429–442.

68   Melnick, H. and Martinez, L. "Preparing teachers to support social and emotional learning: A case study of San Jose State University and Lakewood Elementary School." Palo Alto, CA, Learning Policy Institute, 2019.

69   Konrath, Sara H., Edward H. O'Brien, and Courtney Hsing. "Changes in Dispositional Empathy in American College Students Over Time: A Meta-Analysis." *Personality and Social Psychology Review* (August 5, 2010). https://doi.org/10.1177/1088868310377395.

70   Borba, *UnSelfie.*

71   "2019 State of Workplace Empathy." Businesssolver. Accessed September 23, 2020. https://info.businessolver.com/empathy-2019-executive-summary.

72   Bariso, Jason. "There Are Actually 3 Types of Empathy. Here's How They Differ—and How You Can Develop Them." Inc. September 19, 2018. https://www.inc.com/justin-bariso/there-are-actually-3-types-of-empathy-heres-how-they-differ-and-how-you-can-develop-them-all.html.

73   Walters, Glenn D., and Dorothy L. Espelage. "Cognitive/Affective Empathy, Pro-Bullying Beliefs, and Willingness to Intervene on Behalf of a Bullied Peer." *Youth & Society.* https://doi.org/10.1177/0044118X19858565.

74   Iacoboni, Marco. "Imitation, Empathy, and Mirror Neurons." *Annual Review of Psychology* 60 (2009): 653–70.

75   Keltner, Dacher. *Born to Be good: The Science of a Meaningful Life.* New York: W. W. Norton & Company, 2009.

76   Neff, Kristen. *Self-Compassion: The Proven Power of Being Kind to Yourself.* New York: William Morrow Paperbacks, 2015.

77   Jones, Stephanie M., Suzanne M. Bouffard, and Richard Weissbourd. "Educators' social

and emotional skills vital to learning." *Phi Delta Kappan*, no. 8 (May 2013). http://www.nationalresilienceresource.com/Education/Educators_social_and_emotional_skills.pdf.

78   Torres, Julia. "Building Relationships Linguistically: Using Code Switching to Meet Students On Their Cultural Turf." Imaginarium. Accessed September 24, 2020.

79   Emdin, Christopher. *For White Folks Who Teach in the Hood…and the Rest of Y'all Too: Reality Pedagogy and Urban Education*. Boston, MA: Beacon Press, 2017.

80   Goleman, Daniel. *Focus: The Hidden Driver of Excellence*. New York: Bloomsbury Publishing, 2013.

81   Bach, Dorothe, and Ram Eiseneberg. "'Thinking Where Words are Still Missing': Radical Listening as a Tool to Promote Creative Thinking and Interactional Self-Reliance." 6th Annual Conference on Higher Education Pedagogy, Virginia Tech 2014.

82   Simmons, Dena. "Why We Can't Afford Whitewashed Social Emotional Learning." *ASCD Education Update* 61, no. 4 (April 2019). http://www.ascd.org/publications/newsletters/education_update/apr19/vol61/num04/Why_We_Can't_Afford_Whitewashed_Social-Emotional_Learning.aspx.

83   Martínez, Lorea. "Supporting Teachers' Development of Educational Practices that Attend to Both Students' Cognitive and Social-Emotionl Needs." Universitat Autònoma de Barcelona. 2014.

84   Jagers, Robert J., Deborah Rivas-Drake, and Teresa Borowski. "Equity and Social and Emotional Learning: A Cultural Analysis." *Measuring SEL*. November 2018. https://casel.org/wp-content/uploads/2020/04/equity-and-SEL-.pdf.

85   Fletcher, Jill. "A Framework for Whole-Class Discussions." *Edutopia*. May 7, 2019. https://www.edutopia.org/article/framework-whole-class-discussions.

86   Damon, William. *The Path to Purpose: How Young People Find Their Calling in Life*. New York: Simon & Schuster, 2009.

87   Twenge, Jean M., A. Bell Cooper, Thomas E. Joiner, Mary E. Duffy, and Sarah G. Binau. "Age, period, and cohort trends in mood disorder indicators and sucide-related outcomes in nationally represented dataset, 2015-2017." *Journal of Abnormal Psychology* 128, no. 3 (April 2019): 185–199. https://doi.org/10.1037/abn0000410.

88   Villeneuve, Jennifer C., Jerusha O'Conner, Samantha Selby, and Denise Clark Hope. "Easing the stress at pressure-cooker schools." *Phi Delta Kappan*. October 28, 2019. https://kappanonline.org/easing-stress-pressure-cooker-schools-villeneuve-conner-selby-pope/.

89   "Stress in America: Are Teens Adopting Adults' Stress Habits?" American Psychological Association. 2014. https://www.apa.org/news/press/releases/stress/2013/stress-report.pdf.

90   Damon, *The Path to Purpose*.

91   Martínez, Lorea, and Susan Stillman. "Guiding Youth to Noble Goals: A Practitioner Perspective." *Journal of Character Education* 15, no. 2 (2019): 91–102.

92   Malin, Heather, Timothy S. Reilly, Brandy Quinn, and Seana Moran. "Adolescent purpose development: Exploring empathy, discovering roles, shifting priorities, and creating pathways." *Journal of Research on Adolescence* 24, no. 1 (2014): 186–199. https://doi.org/10.1111/jora.12051.

93   Hatchimonji, Danielle R., Arielle C. Linsky, and Maurci J. Elias. "Fronteirs in Youth Pur-

pose Research." *Journal of Character Education* 15, no. 2 (July 1, 2009). https://www.questia.com/read/1P4-2309266995/special-issue-guest-editors-introduction-frontiers.

94   Jagers, "Equity and Social and Emotional Learning."

95   Borba, *UnSelfie.*

96   Watts Roderick J., Matthew A. Diemer, and Adam M. Voight. "Critical consciousness: current status and future directions." *New Directions for Child and Adolescent Development* 134   (Winter 2011): 43–57. https://doi.org/10.1002/cd.310.

97   Behrendt, Marc, and Teresa Franklin. "A Review of Research on School Field Trips and Their Value in Education." *International Journal of Environmental and Science Education* 9, no. 3 (2014): 235–245.

98   Yoder, Nick, Jordan Posamentier, Dana Godek, Katherine Seibel, and Linda Dusenbury. "From Response to Reopening: State Efforts to Elevate Social and Emotional Learning During the Pandemic." Collaborative for Academic, Social, and Emotional Learning (CASEL). 2020.

99   Bartlett, Jessica Dym, and Rebecca Vivrette. "Ways to Promote Children's Resilience to the COVID-19 Pandemic." Child Trends. April 3, 2020. https://www.childtrends.org/publications/ways-to-promote-childrens-resilience-to-the-covid-19-pandemic.

Chapter 6: HEART Skills in the Virtual Classroom

Moments of crisis and uncertainty, like the one caused by COVID-19, call upon us to support our students and communities, especially those that have been most harmed by disruptions to schools and work, in ways that we didn't anticipate. Before the pandemic, no one expected that many teachers would start the 2020-21 school year virtually, instead of welcoming their students in person. Yet, that is what happened.

During this global pandemic, it is critically important that *we lead our efforts with SEL* and continue to nurture emotional connections with our students, despite the physical distancing. In fact, many states have identified the well-being of students and adults as a top priority in their COVID-19 responses, particularly for those who are most vulnerable and have been disenfranchised.[100]

Teachers have been tasked not only to transition their classrooms to a virtual or hybrid environment, but also to do it in a way that effectively supports the mental health of students who have been impacted by the pandemic—isolation, economic hardship, racial inequities, and stress create a heightened risk for children and adults to experience trauma.[101]

Most teachers are trying to figure out how to proactively address this trauma, while effectively teach academic content, create a sense of community, and maintain their own sanity. As we have noted, the HEART in Mind model can serve as a powerful tool in creating a positive learning environment that supports students as they connect, share, and learn in a virtual community.

A HEART-FILLED VIRTUAL CLASSROOM

Every summer, I teach a course on emotional intelligence to aspiring principals at Teachers College, Columbia University. During the summer of 2020, we had to transition our three-day class to a six-module online course. Before we revised the syllabus, I felt overwhelmed and unprepared. "How are we going to adapt all our experiential, hands-on activities to a virtual environment?" I remember asking myself for weeks.

As you have probably experienced, teaching in an online environment doesn't feel the same than being in a physical space with your students. Are you worried about students feeling disconnected and disengaged? I know many teachers are. The screen can become a barrier to connecting with your students, and an obstacle to support their learning, unless you *intentionally* plan to "humanize the relationship with distant learners."[102]

Based on my experience with the emotional intelligence course, it is possible to create a joyful and supportive virtual classroom. These are some important lessons that I learned:

1. **Focus on building connections with your students.** In a virtual environment, we cannot walk around the playground or stop by the cafeteria during lunch. However, we can still find ways to build relationships with students by communicating more regularly with them and by using different methods. In addition to your morning meeting, you can create videos—showing your pet or sharing a favorite hobby—for your students to watch on their own time. You can write individual emails, give students a call, or invite them to join you during office hours for a one-on-one conversation. The goal is for students to know that you personally care for their well-being.

2. **Offer students a variety of strategies for participating and learning during remote instruction.** It is important that you monitor students' engagement during their synchronous time—when you are all together—and their asynchronous time—when student are doing work on their own. The goal is to make sure students have an opportunity to participate and learn in equal terms, adding their voices and perspectives to the conversation. For some students, this might mean using the chat feature instead of answering a question in front of the whole class; for others it may mean using music and art to communicate their learning, instead of writing an essay. In addition, consider what this may mean for students who don't have the technology resources to fully participate in your classroom. Are there other ways in which you can bring their voice into the classroom? For additional strategies, read the article "8 Strategies to Improve Participation in Your Virtual Classroom" written by *Edutopia's* assistant editor, Emmelina Minero.[103]

3. **Be intentional and apply your empathy.** In a distance learning environment, it is important to consider students' needs when you plan your teaching—ask yourself, "Why am I giving students this reading or writing assignment? How is it going to support their engagement in my classroom?" Many teachers would agree that teaching during and after a pandemic is all about putting "Maslow before Bloom." That is to say, focusing on students' basic needs, such as the need to feel safe and having a sense of belonging in your classroom—before you dive into academics. Think about your teaching—the ways in which you engage students during videoconferences, the kinds of assignments you create, the way your Google Classroom is structured—from your students' perspectives. How would it feel going through a day in the life of one of your students? By applying your empathy, you may find ways to connect more deeply with your students and work toward becoming a more effective online teacher.

4. **Ask for feedback.** Although you may be checking in with your students on a regular basis already, it might be helpful to gather information about how things are going in a more formal way. Use

one of the many survey tools available—SurveyMonkey, Google Forms, Brightspace—to ask students for feedback about specific assignments or projects and the virtual classroom in general. Asking for feedback can feel vulnerable and scary—I understand, I've been there—but it's a worthy exercise. Students often have great ideas for how things could be improved, and they're very tech savvy! Asking for feedback is also a way to develop students' metacognition skills, as it encourages them to think about how they learn best.

5. **Celebrate and share what is working**. Transitioning to a virtual learning environment is not easy. Remember to acknowledge and celebrate the things that are working, big and small. Share these small wins with your colleagues, so you can continue to learn from each other as you navigate the challenges of teaching during and after a pandemic.

TEACHING REMOTELY WITH THE HEART IN MIND

Our emotional lives have been greatly impacted by the pandemic—young people and adults have felt stress, fear, grief, and a sense of being overwhelmed at levels they may have not experienced in the past. In our virtual environment, HEART skills can become powerful tools for students to build their resilience, connect with others, and develop a sense of agency.

Honor Your Emotions

When we experience big emotions and don't have the tools to manage them effectively, we cannot learn or focus. Creating time and space to check in with your students and see how they are feeling becomes essential during distance learning. Don't skip your morning check-in! It sets up the tone for the day and helps students transition from the home environment to the virtual classroom. Use apps like Mood Meter, Padlet, or Mentimeter to help students name their emotions and create a visual representation of the data. As students are encouraged to connect with their emotions, they gain valuable information to guide their behaviors.

Elect Your Responses

Keeping students focused and away from distractions during remote learning is challenging—students can be looking straight into the camera while concentrating completely on a task unrelated to your classroom's instruction. In addition to helping students develop tools to regulate their emotions—mindful breathing, naming their feelings, taking a break—discussed as part of Elect Your Responses in Chapter Five, it's important to teach students effective ways to manage their time and get organized. They can benefit from using tools that help them stay on track; even simple steps like using timers, printing calendars with assignments, choosing a buddy to check on them, and closing all tabs when they are in a Zoom call or Google Hangout will support students' executive functioning skills. The goal is not on compliance, but on keeping students engaged and aware of the distractions they face.

Apply Empathy

The pandemic has disproportionally impacted schools in underserved communities; racially motivated murders and police brutality are occurring within this context. An increased awareness about how other people—especially those from diverse backgrounds and cultures—are experiencing this situation has caused schools and educators to examine the racist practices and deficit-based thinking embedded in our systems.[104] As you are engaging with students during remote learning, create the space for students to process current events and how these are impacting their own and other communities. By learning about different perspectives, we develop our capacity for empathy and develop tools to navigate adversity.

Reignite Your Relationships

It's possible to maintain healthy and supportive relationships in the distance learning classroom. Although educators are provided more limited and restricted opportunities to interact with students, they are also given a window into students' home lives and direct communication with parents and caregivers. This is a new situation for all—students, teachers, and parents—to navigate, so it may take some trial and error until you find the right balance. Start by maximizing the impact of your interactions with students—prioritize getting to know them, establish positive connections, and stay present and available for students. As noted earlier, using a variety of tools to build these relationships with students can support you in creating a sense of community and belonging in your classroom.

Transform with Purpose

As students try to navigate distance learning during a pandemic, cultivating a sense of purpose may contribute to students' resilience. In this context, having purpose means that we recognize our ability to do something for the betterment of our families and communities, even in small doses. Engaging students in project-based and service learning can help to ignite their curiosity, develop their empathy, and improve their engagement during your remote instruction, just as they are developing ways to contribute to others and advocate for themselves.

In Chapter Five we explored many strategies and activities that you can use to teach and integrate the HEART in Mind model in your classroom. *Many of these tools can be adapted and used effectively in a virtual setting.* For example:

- You can adapt how students engage during the activity by changing from a pair-share to a small break out room during remote instruction.

- You can switch the in-person direct instruction to a recorded video if you want students to watch during their asynchronous time.

- You can have students record a personal reflection about a lesson, book, or video instead of reading or sharing from their reflection journals.

No matter how you adapt the tools, *it is essential that you continue to bring these HEART skills into your classroom by actively teaching and integrating them into your practice.* Even in a virtual environment, you can foster strong and positive relationships with your students—remember that these meaningful relationships can mitigate the negative effects of trauma and mental health concerns in the short and long term. Checking in with your students to ask how they are feeling, providing them with tools to regulate their emotions, and helping them to connect with their peers can go a long way toward supporting their mental health and ability to learn. Don't give up!

Endnotes

100   Moore, Michael, and Greg Kearsley. *Distance Education: A Systems View of Online Learning*. Boston, MA: Cengage Learning, 2011.

101   Minero, Emelina. "8 Strategies to Improve Participation in Your Virtual Classroom." *Edutopia*. August 21, 2020. https://www.edutopia.org/article/8-strategies-improve-participation-your-virtual-classroom.

102   Cipriano, Christina, Gabrielle Rappolt-Schlichtmann, and Marc Brackett. "Supporting School Community Wellness with Social and Emotional Learning (SEL) During and After a Pandemic." PennState College of Health and Human Development. August 2020. https://www.prevention.psu.edu/uploads/files/PSU-SEL-Crisis-Brief.pdf.

103   Dewey, John. *Experience and Education*. New York: Free Press, 1997 (reprint).

104   Martínez, Lorea, and Hannah Melnick. "Preparing Teachers to Support Social and Emotional Learning." Learning Policy Institute. May 21, 2019. https://learningpolicyinstitute.org/product/social-and-emotional-learning-case-study-san-jose-state-report.

Chapter 7: Integrating HEART Skills into Academic Lessons

Students will not be able to achieve mastery of academic content if they feel bored, stressed, or isolated; they will not be able to focus on learning or remember any of the content presented in class. Knowing the importance of emotions in learning, we aim to create a classroom environment where the emotional needs of students are met and they feel connected, activated, energized, and are eager and able to engage with academic content in deeper ways.

An important part of teaching with the HEART in Mind is to analyze how you can effectively and efficiently integrate this model into your academic lessons, so these skills not only come alive in your teaching but also support students' emotional and cognitive needs, which will lead to better outcomes.

In my experience working with schools, the explicit instruction part of the SEL implementation process is generally a prime concern and a well thought-out plan by those who make budgetary and instructional decisions. The part that does not receive that much attention is the infusion with academics. Somehow, teachers are supposed to figure it out on their own without any additional planning time or targeted support.

Infusing HEART skills into academic lessons is less about finding the "right key" and more about using a variety of tools to make learning more meaningful and engaging.

To make this happen, teachers have a secret weapon—lesson planning. Teachers spend a good amount of time planning with their teams, looking for visual resources, creating rubrics, and setting up classroom projects. Given the time that teachers *already* spend on lessons, why not use it to make sure HEART skills are clearly articulated and infused in the lesson plan?

To make the integration of HEART skills into academic lessons easier, I have developed a three-step process. First, we look at lesson plan design from an SEL perspective. Second, we identify the HEART skills that students will need to access the content, engage with the activities and master the learning goal. Third, we look for ways to connect the academic content with HEART skills. Let's dig in.

STEP 1: LOOKING AT LESSON PLAN DESIGN

You are probably familiar with "backward design" for creating content units and courses. With this approach, you consider the learning goals of a course and determine how students will be assessed first, before thinking about how to teach the content and which activities students will be doing.[105] In this first step, you go through a similar process by looking at your lesson design with HEART skills in mind and what you know about good teaching. There are four core components in the structure of a lesson:

1. **Aim:** The aim reflects your desired outcome: what you expect students to learn by the end of your lesson or unit of study. In many cases, this aim will be informed by your state or country standards and will be connected to a particular content area (mathematics, language, social sciences). My suggestion is that you add a social and emotional learning goal that supports the academic content. This could be connected to a skill in the HEART in Mind model that you would like your students to develop as they are learning the academic skills and knowledge. For example, you could select one of the indicators of mastery that we have reviewed in Chapter Five. It could also be a goal that involves more than one skill.

You should share these social and emotional goals the same way that you share your academic goals with your students. This way, students know what they should pay attention to as they engage with the content and the different activities that you present.

Take a look at these examples:

> Academic Aim: Students will describe how a story plot unfolds and how the characters respond or change overtime (Common Core, reading/language 6.3).

> HEART Aim: Students will explain their behavior patterns and things that trigger certain emotions and behaviors (Elect Your Responses, strategic learner).

> Academic Aim: Students will identify alternative ways to solve complex problems (mathematics standards).

> HEART Aim: Students will use active listening skills and will disagree with others in constructive ways (Reignite Your Relationships, advanced beginner).

Indicators:

- The lesson has an academic objective along with a social and emotional goal or area of focus.
- These goals are shared with students.

2. **Hook**: The hook is something you introduce at the beginning of a lesson to engage students and draw their attention. It could be done through posing a provocative question, showing an inspiring video, or doing a short activity. The hook is the teacher's way to get students to be more emotionally involved in the learning process, so they *want to* see and experience what is coming next.

A hook should be related to the content and skills you will be teaching or should build upon students' interests and personal experiences. The goal is to create an "emotional climate" in the classroom that aligns with the lesson. For example, if students are going to be writing a personal story, your opening activity should help students look inward and keep a lower energy level. On the other hand, if students are going to be using different materials to build a prototype, you might want the hook to increase your students' energy levels so they are ready to work in groups.

Indicators:

- The lesson plan starts with a hook to engage students and draw their attention (question, video, short activity).

- The hook builds connections with the content and/or among students.

- The hook creates an "emotional climate" in the classroom that aligns with the lesson.

3. **Mobilize**: This section includes your mini-lesson and opportunities for student practice. As the name indicates, this is a time where you want students to be fully active, engaging their minds, hands, and hearts. There are many things that you can do to be culturally responsive and keep students emotionally engaged and invested in learning. The following indicators, which we have reviewed throughout this book, are examples of key elements that should be present in your lessons.

Indicators:

- The lesson incorporates physical movement.

- The lesson incorporates different ways to deliver information (auditory, visual, tactile).

- The lesson is divided into chunks and includes attention-focused activities or brain breaks.

- Students have choices about the ways in which they show understanding or complete the tasks.

- The lesson materials are culturally responsive and reflect students' social and cultural identities.

- The lesson builds on classroom routines and also incorporates novelty to keep students engaged.

4. **Consolidate:** American philosopher and educational reformer John Dewey claimed that we don't learn from experience, we learn from reflecting on experience.[106]Reflecting helps us to clarify what was learned and, hopefully, it will inspire new thoughts and actions. Consolidate is probably the most important part of the learning process, and one that we often skip due to ongoing time constraints in the classroom. During this stage, students make sense of what they have learned by reflecting on their experience, how it confirms or questions what they already know, and the ways in which they can use the new skills or knowledge to accomplish their personal and academic goals. This step in the process prepares them to develop new learning. Consolidation activities will vary depending on your students, the desired lesson outcome, and the amount of time you have available. These are some examples to get you started:

> **Journaling.** Students (and educators) may record activities, thoughts, feelings, and questions in an individual or group journal. Depending on what you'd like students to focus on during these reflective times, you may ask specific questions about what they learned that day or broader questions regarding their learning experience and the things they would like to improve, moving forward. This could also be a time for free writing.

> **Group discussion.** Listening and speaking are also ways to reflect, and they enhance students' HEART skills. You can facilitate discussions focused on the content and skills students are learning in your class or how they plan to apply them toward other projects in class or outside of school. These shared spaces can assist learners in making sense of their learning and the learning of others. They can also provide teachers with meaningful data that can be used to modify and differentiate future lessons. For example, an interesting discussion could emerge from:

> o I used to think . . .

> o Now I think . . .

> **Art.** Some students might prefer to express their feelings or thoughts visually rather than verbally or in writing. Offer students

the chance to draw, paint, or build as a way to reflect about themselves and their learning.

Indicators:

- The lesson incorporates exit tickets, sharing opportunities, or reflection questions.

- The lesson has opportunities for students to connect their learning with real life.

Aim	The lesson has an academic objective along with a social and emotional goal or area of focus.
	These goals are shared with students.
Hook	The lesson plan starts with a hook to engage students and draw their attention (question, video, short activity).
	The hook builds connections with the content and/or among students.
	The hook creates an "emotional climate" in the classroom that aligns with the lesson.
Mobilize	The lesson incorporates physical movement.
	The lesson incorporates different ways to deliver information (auditory, visual, tactile).
	The lesson is divided into chunks and includes attention-focused activities or brain breaks.
	Students have choices about the ways in which they show understanding or complete the tasks.
	The lesson materials are culturally responsive and reflect students' social and cultural identities.
	The lesson builds on classroom routines and also incorporates novelty to keep students engaged.
Consolidate	The lesson incorporates exit tickets, sharing opportunities, or reflection questions.
	The lesson has opportunities for students to connect their learning with real life.

STEP 2: IDENTIFYING THE HEART SKILLS STUDENTS NEED

In 2019, I published a case study with the Learning Policy Institute about how teachers can be supported in teaching SEL.[107] One of the fifth-grade teachers in the study shared how, partway into the first semester, she realized her students were having a hard time working in teams. Problems with teamwork were hindering their ability to engage in science activities in which students were asked to summarize an article as a group. In this case, students had a hard time working together because they did not know each other well. In order to support students in their academic teamwork, the teacher implemented a series of activities to help students get to know each other during morning meeting, and she created a sense of community through different team-building activities. Her students needed additional support with their HEART skills—particularly with Apply Empathy and Reignite Your Relationships—in order to fully engage with the activities and meet the learning goal.

In this second infusion step, you identify the HEART skills that students will need in order to *access* the content, *engage* with the activities, and *reach* the learning goal. Once you know what those skills are, think about places where students might need additional support:

Intrapersonal Skills	**H**	Honor Your Emotions	Naming, interpreting, and appropriately communicating feelings
	E	Elect Your Responses	Creating space to make constructive and safe decisions
Interpersonal Skills	**A**	Apply Empathy	Recognizing and valuing the emotions and perspectives of others and taking action to support them. Nurturing self-compassion
	R	Reignite Your Relationships	Nurturing a positive and supportive network by actively using communication and conflict-resolution skills and working cooperatively with diverse individuals and groups
Cognitive Skills	**T**	Transform with Purpose	Using personal assets and interests to positively contribute to self and others

- Would you change any of the activities based on students' current HEART skills?

- Would you add any additional supports/scaffolding?

- Are there any HEART skills not infused in the lesson that should be there?

- If yes, when and how could you incorporate them?

STEP 3: CONNECTING CONTENT WITH HEART SKILLS

During the first two steps of infusing the HEART in Mind model into academic lessons, we looked at how HEART skills can support and improve students' engagement with the lesson and their mastery of the academic content. In this third step, it is the other way around—we look at the content itself and find out if there are any connections that can be made to HEART skills. For example, you can highlight social and emotional skills by recognizing when people in the news, social media, or our community use (or don't use) these skills. Imagine you are reading *I Am Malala*, Malala Yousfzai's harrowing tale of her family uprooted by global terrorism and her personal fight for the education rights of girls around the world. In your discussion of the book, you could ask your students:

- How does she feel? (Honor Your Emotions)

- What are/were her choices? (Elect Your Responses)

- What is her purpose? (Transform with Purpose)

By highlighting the specific competencies that Malala displays, students start to develop the capacity to recognize these important skills in other people. By paying attention to those elements, we are sending a clear message to students—these are skills worth paying attention to.

Another example would be in solving multistep math problems, something that many students struggle to do. Before you start the lesson, you could discuss some of the emotional reactions to these kinds of problems. You can share your own pleasant or unpleasant experience with them, which models Honor Your Emotions; if we want students to be open about their feelings, we need to be able to share our feelings too. Then, introduce (or review) some self-talk strategies that they can use if they start feeling frustrated or scared, reinforcing the skills of Elect Your Responses. What can students tell themselves when they get stuck? Students can brainstorm or you can provide them with ideas. Taking a deep breath, rereading the problem and finding out what they know, or just taking one step at a time are a few strategies that could help students reengage with the task by applying the skills of Elect Your Responses.

Teaching with the HEART in Mind helps educators to teach better. By looking at lesson designs, identifying places where students may need additional support to use their HEART skills, and connecting content with these skills, teachers can become pros at infusing SEL into academic lessons.

Based on the work that we have done so far, use these prompts to reflect on your classroom and teaching practices:

- How am I amplifying opportunities to apply HEART skills in my lesson?

- How am I appealing to students' emotions and social and cultural identities in my teaching?

- I don't see an opportunity to connect HEART skills in this lesson. Is it worth teaching?

- How am I communicating the HEART skills needed to reach academic goals to my students?

- How am I planning to develop the HEART skills needed to access and engage with the academic content?

- When students don't perform as I expected, am I considering both the academic and HEART skills (or lack of) that may get in the way of learning?

- When students don't perform as I expected, how am I reflecting on my teaching practice?

- How am I helping students develop the HEART skills needed to know each other and work well together?

- How am I nurturing trust and belonging in the classroom?

- What tools and strategies am I using to support students' physical and emotional safety?

- How am I providing behavioral supports that improve students' engagement and growth?
- How am I making myself available and present for when students need to talk to an adult?

Endnotes

105   Bowen, Ryan S. "Understanding by Design." Vanderbilt University Center for Teaching, 2017. Retrieved from https://cft.vanderbilt.edu/understanding-by-design/.

106   McGonigal, Kelly. *The Upside of Stress: Why Stress is Good For You, And How to Get Good at It*. New York: Avery, 2016.

107   Mader, Jackie. "As schools reopen, are teachers OK? COVID, stress, new rules, regulations and more add to anxiety." *Northern Kentucky Tribune*. August 17, 2020.

PART 3: THE WHOLE-HEARTED EDUCATOR

Working with educators is probably my favorite part of the job. The teachers that I have worked with are committed, passionate, and courageous. They want to get better at teaching because they care for their students' well-being and success, and they are willing to do the HEART work to examine their teaching practices in service of equity. They are "a force for good." Every time I work with teachers, I am reminded that supporting the social and emotional growth of adults, children, and youth is doing the work that matters. It touches human hearts with long-lasting effects. It is time well spent.

But our teachers are not all right. A survey launched by the Yale Center for Emotional Intelligence and the Collaborative for Social Emotional and Academic Learning (CASEL) found that *anxious, fearful, worried, overwhelmed,* and *sad* were the five most-mentioned emotions among over 5,000 US teachers during the COVID-19 crisis.[108] If experienced for an extended period of time, these feelings can negatively impact teachers' mental health and worsen teacher burnout during and after the pandemic.

Stanford psychologist and author of the book *The Upside of Stress*, Dr. Kelly McGonigal, argues that focusing on the reasons that brought teachers to the teaching profession can alleviate these difficult feelings and provide some relief in navigating these uncertain and challenging situations.[109]

Many teachers start their careers with a deep love for learning and hopes for a better future; maybe they want to provide kids with opportunities they did not have when they were growing up, or they feel a commitment to help others who were born in disadvantaged circumstances. When I was in high school in Catalunya, I volunteered to help newly immigrated North-African women. Knowing nothing about how to teach, I taught Spanish classes, helping the women to read and have everyday conversations. We talked about their traditions and the struggles to adjust to a new land with a different culture, language, and religion. Many of them were happy to be there but missed their home country. My parents had also moved—from the northeastern part of Spain to the town where I grew up in Catalunya—and shared these same feelings. They felt as if they were between two places, neither here nor there. This experience taught me that my family and I had many things in common with these women, a shared experience with similar feelings, despite different circumstances. Unfortunately, the value that I saw in knowing and welcoming these women was not shared by the other citizens in my hometown. There was tension and fear between the two groups (locals versus immigrants), even hate. This is when I decided to dedicate my life to education.

What about you? What brought you to teaching? Why were you drawn to the classroom? To center our conversation about this "whole-hearted" educator, who teaches with the HEART in Mind, and is able to face the challenges of our current times, we need to discuss purpose. Purpose is the compass that guides our actions and the choices we make, and it is the light that will help us keep going when things get difficult. I would like to invite you to reflect on these two questions. Write it down on a piece of paper or a Post-it if it is helpful.

- Why does the work I do matter to me?

- How does my work impact the lives of others?

The work of teaching and being in the classroom is exhausting, messy, and stressful. It often feels like pushing a huge boulder; we keep trying and pushing, but the rock does not move. The COVID-19 crisis has shed a light on the urgency of supporting the social and emotional needs of educators, "recognizing they are going to be experiencing a great deal of vicarious trauma."[110] During the pandemic, teachers not only experience their own trauma, but also take on the additional stress from supporting students who have been impacted by this global crisis. While we want teachers to be connected with their purpose, educational systems need to invest in creating systemic and systematic SEL initiatives that include supporting the HEART skills of educators and staff working with children and youth. Otherwise, we'll continue to see the departure of about 200,000 teachers a year who leave the profession due to challenging working conditions, lack of support, and poor pay.[111]

We cannot think about adults' HEART skills as something to do or address when schools' SEL programs are up and running. The thing is that *unless* we support adults in growing their social and emotional capacity, students and the learning environment will be greatly impacted.[112]

- **Teachers' social and emotional competencies influence the quality of teacher-student relationships.** Teachers who are calm, positive, and content are likely to be better equipped for treating students warmly and sensitively, even when students behave in challenging ways.

- **Teachers model these skills, intentionally or not.** Teachers navigate stressful situations every day—and students are paying attention! They learn from how their teachers deal with conflicts or maintain control of the classroom, and whether or not they foster a prosocial classroom climate.

- **Teachers' social and emotional skills influence classroom organization and management.** Teachers must maintain a sense of calm, be organized, and cultivate social trust if they want a well-organized classroom that encourages creativity and student autonomy.

As you can see, it is crucial that educators practice their HEART skills for two essential reasons: First, so they can develop their resilience and do the work they love for the long term. Second, so they can model and teach these skills to their students and become more effective educators. This generally does not happen from one day to the next; the same way that athletes practice to improve their skills, educators need *intentional* practice to become more effective and resilient teachers in the long run. The next three chapters are written to help you with this process.

Endnotes

108   Podolsky, Anne, Tara Kini, Joseph Bishop, and Linda Darling-Hammond. "Solving the Teacher Shortage: How to Retain Excellent Educators." Learning Policy Institute. September 15, 2016. https://learningpolicyinstitute.org/product/solving-teacher-shortage.

109   Jones, Stephanie M., Suzanne M. Bouffard, and Richard Weissbourd. "Educators' social and emotional skills vital to learning." *Phi Delta Kappan,* no. 8 (May 2013). http://www.nationalresilienceresource.com/Education/Educators_social_and_emotional_skills.pdf.

110   Jennings, Patricia A., Sebrina Doyle, Yoonkyung Oh, Damira Rasheed, Jennifer L. Frank, and Joshua L. Brown. "Long-term impacts of the CARE program on teachers' self-reported social and emotional competence and well-being." *Journal of School Psychology* 76 (October 2019): 186–202.

111   Schussler, Deborah L., Patricia A. Jennings, Jennifer E. Sharp, and Jennifer L. Frank. "Improving Teacher Awareness and Well-Being Through CARE: a Qualitative Analysis of the underlying Mechanisms." *Mindfulness* 7 (2016): 130–142.

112   Bergeisen, Michael. "The Neuroscience of Happiness." *Greater Good Magazine.* September 22, 2010. https://greatergood.berkeley.edu/article/item/the_neuroscience_of_happiness.

Chapter 8: Finding Your Voice

SEL is as much about knowing yourself as an educator as it is about knowing how to teach and infuse HEART skills in the classroom. It is when we (educators) notice our emotions and elect our responses that we create the space to make more conscious decisions that support students' learning and growth.

Sometimes examining our HEART skills brings some unexpected insights that may be difficult to process. Let me illustrate. I met Angela when I was teaching a course for aspiring principals in New Orleans, Louisiana. After doing some work on emotional literacy and relationships, Angela realized that while she was an effective teacher and children generally liked her, she put less effort into developing relationships with adults, which impacted her ability to be seen as a leader at the school. She identified the reason, but had a hard time accepting that she would need to "do the work" to create positive relationships with others. In her case, it was mostly about acknowledging that adults had feelings too and creating the space for those emotions to exist in the relationship. She hoped that each adult would keep their feelings to themselves, so they could just focus on the work at hand. The thing is, we cannot escape our emotions or the emotions of others. Angela needed to practice tolerating a sense of discomfort when others shared their feelings.

She struggled with this for several weeks, and it was not until we had our last session together that she was able to take a step and try a different way of relating to others. It took an enormous amount of courage—being outside of her comfort zone and trying out behaviors that were new to her—but she did it, putting herself on a different path with more awareness about herself and others, which positively impacted her ability to build relationships. Ultimately, she would become a better leader because of this.

PRACTICING THE HEART IN MIND MODEL

> *"My experience in the SEL course was transformational in ways that I was not at all anticipating when I began the program, and has really had a lasting impact on the way I live my life and navigate the world."*
> —*Teacher, New Orleans, Louisiana*

Engaging in this type of process requires educators to be courageous; there is a degree of vulnerability that comes with acknowledging that we are not perfect, that there is room for improvement in our operating system. Dr. Brené Brown, author and research professor at the University of Houston, says, "Courage starts with showing up and letting ourselves be seen." This *showing up* may look different for Angela (my former student), your partner teacher, or yourself. Based on our social identities, culture, religion, or life experiences, we put these HEART skills into practice differently; we often hide behind a mask because we are afraid of letting others see our authentic selves. As we have discussed, there is value in unpacking and listening to these feelings so we can discover what we are afraid of and what would happen if we weren't.

What would you do if you weren't afraid?

Another teacher in Angela's course, Tiffany, was contemplating what to do after finishing her administrative credential. She shared, "There is fear for me in the unknowing and in doing what feels like wavering from the path I expected to take, but I know that fear means this matters to me immensely—not that this is the wrong decision."

When we pay attention to our emotions, we gain new insights that help us to make better decisions and that sometimes lead us to alternative paths that we had thought not possible. Tiffany started her administrative credential thinking that she would become a school administrator when she was done; as she completed her coursework, she found herself considering other paths. Although she felt scared, she knew that there was something to learn from this feeling if she let herself listen to it.

When teachers engage in this work, with a balance of support and challenge, they feel more satisfied and better prepared to face the emotional challenges that come with teaching. In recent years, a number of SEL and mindfulness-based interventions have shown great results in promoting well-being and reducing stress levels among healthy adults.[113] For example, the Cultivating Awareness and Resilience in Education (CARE) program, developed by Dr. Tish Jennings and colleagues, showed significant decreases in teachers' psychological distress, reductions in ache-related physical distress, and a continuation of significant increases in emotion regulation and some dimensions of mindfulness.[114] In addition, teachers in this study reported sustained and new benefits regarding their well-being even one year after the program had been completed. As you read in the opening quote of this section, this work has long-lasting benefits.

Although any teacher can take steps to develop their social and emotional capacity, having the right kinds of supports is essential in increasing educators' effectiveness and maintaining their well-being in the long term. In certain cases, teachers will be able to clearly see which HEART skills they are underutilizing and which ones they are using effectively. In most cases, educators need intrapersonal and interpersonal skills, sustained effort— building stamina through a cycle of reflection, action, and reflection—and other people to help them unpack some of their learned behaviors and begin to adopt new practices.

How do you get started? As you have probably noticed, HEART skills have indicators of mastery for the "Practicing Expert" category—this refers to individuals who are in college or beyond, which includes all the adults. Being a practicing expert means that we have a solid foundation for each competency and can continually use these skills in our different personal and professional communities.

Honor Your Emotions

- Identifies how emotions affect decision-making and interprets their meaning
- Evaluates how expressing emotions affects others and communicates accordingly
- Generates ways to use emotions to accomplish personal goals

Elect Your Responses

- Adjusts behavior and emotions in response to changes in the environment or to changes in one's goals
- Uses tools and strategies to transform unproductive patterns
- Generates alternative solutions to problems and sustains optimism

Apply Empathy

- Demonstrates understanding of those who have different emotions and perspectives
- Demonstrates ways to act and live with compassion
- Generates strategies to nurture self-compassion in daily life

Reignite Your Relationships

- Uses assertive communication to meet needs without negatively impacting others
- Evaluates effectiveness of one's own conflict resolution and negotiation skills and plans how to improve them
- Plans, implements, and leads participation in a group project
- Uses cultural competence and humility in building relationships

Transform with Purpose

- Applies personal interests, values, and strengths to contribute to others
- Analyzes social, economic, and political structures that maintain inequities, and acts to dismantle them

- Monitors progress toward equitable outcomes and living purposefully

Looking at these 16 indicators as a complete list may feel overwhelming, and maybe feel impossible to accomplish in a lifetime. Think about it this way—these indicators are a way to gauge the level or the degree to which you are putting a skill into practice. For example, you may realize that you aren't generally compassionate with yourself (it seems to be common among educators). If that's the case and it is something you would like to develop, you can start working toward adopting one (maybe two) strategies to nurture self-compassion when you have a bad teaching day or you make a mistake. The step of working toward that indicator is practicing your HEART skills; in the process, you will probably use and strengthen other skills within the model. These skills are related and build on each other.

Another thing to consider when looking at these indicators is how our life events impact the ways and the degree to which we use our HEART skills. If we are under a high level of stress due to events such as an unexpected illness in the family, a job transition, or relocating to a new state, our ability to access our social and emotional tools will be impacted. It will be more difficult to use these skills under those circumstances. However, if you commit to developing your HEART capacity and take simple steps to practice these skills—such as adopting mindfulness practices to calm the nervous system—even under stress, you will be more likely to stay calm and keep your focus.

If you are ready to get started, find a quiet place, a pen and paper, and answer the following questions:

1. Identify a problem or need in your personal or professional life that you'd like to address. Is there something related to this issue that you would like to start doing, do better, or change?

2. Are there HEART skills that would help you in this process (i.e., skills that you know you use well?) Any specific indicators? Are there HEART skills that you would need to grow? Any specific indicators?

3. Based on your answers to the questions, what are your next steps? Who can you enlist to support you? What resources will you use?

4. How will you know that you have solved the problem or address the need? What impact will it have on you and/or others?

Practicing HEART skills doesn't necessarily mean making big changes to how we behave or relate to others. Sometimes it is the *awareness* that comes from paying attention to these skills that can bring the greatest results. A few years back, one of my former adult students realized he had negative thoughts when he was presented with a new task or activity, even when the task seemed fun or interesting. He tended to think about feeling dumb or embarrassed, the risks of engaging in the activity, or how long it would take him to learn or perform it. These negative thoughts took all the potential fun out of doing something new, which made him not want to engage in new activities. He was a creature of habit!

After being part of an SEL course, this young man realized how much these negative thoughts and unpleasant emotions impacted his life. He decided to do something about it and took the first step—he started *noticing* when and how these negative thoughts occurred. From the outside, you couldn't see any differences in his behavior; he seemed the same. However, when he started noticing the thoughts and emotions that were pulling him away from fully engaging with his work and life, he was able to tame them by first acknowledging them—not avoiding or ignoring them—and second, by putting them aside—not letting them control his actions. There were still cases when he decided not to engage with certain new activities, but he felt a greater sense of control over his decisions. In other cases, he was able to do them and enjoy the experience.

I hope these true stories illustrate the positive impact that practicing HEART skills can have on adults' professional and personal lives. It is never too early or too late to start practicing them for ourselves and our students; when we have clarity about what it means to grow our own social and emotional capacity, we can better support students doing the same. In the appendix, you will find a self-assessment survey of these HEART skills. Use this tool to understand your strengths and identify areas where you can grow.

FACILITATING WITH HEART IN MIND

When you teach with the HEART in Mind, the way you prepare yourself as a facilitator is an important and necessary step in the implementation process. Some of the conversations that you will have with your students may touch on difficult topics: systemic racism, discrimination, poverty, food insecurity, and the collective trauma and grief experienced by so many families and educators during the pandemic. Some of the activities may require letting go of a final outcome and being more focused on the process of learning. Others may need you to illustrate a skill with a personal story. While it is normal to feel unsure or uncomfortable the first time you teach the HEART skills, you will gain confidence over time and find a way to do it that speaks to who you are as a teacher. There is no "magic bullet" for how you teach these skills. However, there are things that you can do to implement the HEART in Mind model effectively. Let me illustrate using one of my favorite Catalan traditions—*castells*—these are human towers, built as teams of people stand on each other's shoulders at festival competitions in Catalunya. They represent solidarity and team spirit among Catalan people.

The tradition of castells started in Tarragona (one of Spain's four Catalan provinces) at the end of the 18th century when rival groups began to compete with each other in constructing different kinds of human towers. As you can see in the picture, there are different parts to a castell:

- The *pinya* is the horizontal base of the construction where the accumulated weight rests. It's used to stabilize the structure and soften falls if any should occur.

- The *tronc* is the vertical structure that consists of a certain number of people on each level.

- And the top, the crown of the castle, is the *canalla* (which means the youngsters). The last casteller to climb the tower is a young boy or girl, the *anxaneta,* who raises one hand to salute the public.

For this human tower to go up, castellers use *relational trust*, which is based on four key ingredients:

- **Technique**: The individuals who form the horizontal structure need to position themselves in a certain way to balance other bodies on their shoulders. They need to lock arms with their neighbor to keep the structure stable.

- **Strength:** The strength must be both physical, to sustain the weight of the other castellers, and emotional, to manage the stress when things start shaking.

- **Teamwork:** The castellers have to work together in order to make it happen and must support each other when things are not going well.

- **Practice:** Successful castell teams don't occur overnight. Castellers spend hours and hours training and practicing to build their beautiful and strong castells.

These human towers serve as a powerful analogy for our SEL work in schools and classrooms, and they demonstrate how educators can prepare themselves for this work. In order to grow our students' HEART skills, educators need to develop relational trust using these same four ingredients:

Technique: You need to develop fluency in the HEART in Mind model: know the skills, be familiar with the indicators of mastery, know what these skills look like in practice and how you can model them for students. You must also have effective resources and materials, such as the many strategies and activities included in this book.

Strength: You will need strength and courage to overcome challenges. We know that implementing something new is always messy, and valuable lessons can be learned from this process. Remember that courage is not the absence of fear, but our ability to do something that frightens us. In this context, being courageous means being open and honest with ourselves and taking action even when we feel insecure or uncomfortable. To develop your strength, complete your HEART in Mind plan and practice HEART skills every day. Every interaction—with your family, your students, or the cashier at the grocery store—is an opportunity to use your skills.

Teamwork: We can do more when we share our accomplishments and struggles with colleagues; sometimes we lend a hand, sometimes we receive support. Hopefully, you have colleagues at your school that can become your HEART buddies. My dream is that groups of educators will adopt the HEART in Mind model and work together to implement the suggested strategies, adding their own activities and supporting each other along the way. If you don't have colleagues at your school or district, use technology to connect with other like-minded educators. The HEART in Mind Facebook group is one option, but there are many other SEL-related groups online as well.

Practice: In order to feel comfortable facilitating this learning for our students and to be effective, we need to practice and iterate. Sometimes it takes several trials before a lesson meets our learning objective. It is through practice that we can improve our craft, learn from what worked and what didn't, and come up with additional resources. The hardest part is to get started! Once you do, create a routine that will work for you and your students.

Now, think about the SEL work you are doing in your current classroom and reflect on the following questions:

- Which one of these ingredients of relational trust do you embrace the most?

- Why is that ingredient important to you?

- If you decided to develop another ingredient, which one would it be?

- What impact would it have on your HEART facilitation skills and your students if you were able to strengthen it? How would you know that it is working?

MOVING FROM JUDGMENT TO CURIOSITY

When adults practice their HEART skills and prepare themselves to teach them in their classrooms, the ways they perceive and work with children change. I have witnessed this transformation time and time again. Educators move from a deficit-based approach where they are focused on the problems and the needs they cannot address, to a strengths-based approach where they can see the opportunities and benefits of doing this work, using their students' and their own strengths to develop whole-hearted individuals. Teachers also develop more awareness of the ways in which deficit-thinking models are embedded in our educational systems, and they start creating pathways to break out of these mindsets. This transformation is possible when educators engage with this work from a place of curiosity and an open mind, moving away from "can'ts" and "don'ts" to a place of possibilities.

Endnotes

113   Siegel, D. J., *Mindsight: The new science of personal transformation*. New York: Bantam, 2010.

114   Neff, Kristen. *Self-Compassion: The Proven Power of Being Kind to Yourself*. New York: William Morrow Paperbacks, 2015.

Chapter 9: Building Your Resilience

Many teachers come to the profession with a desire to change the odds for disadvantaged students, share their own passions, or create engaging experiences for children. Over time, the working conditions—long hours, lack of support, emotional labor, systemic discriminatory and deficit-based practices—take a toll on teachers' well-being and their ability and desire to stay in the profession for the long term. I have worked with early childhood, elementary, middle school, and high school teachers and administrators across the United States. There is a pattern that repeats time and time again—how greatly teaching impacts educators' well-being and how little support they receive in learning skills and strategies to improve it.

During a training session, a high school teacher shared with me: "When I am in school, I give it my all. By the time I get home, I have nothing else to give." She also shared that she spent at least three hours every night checking and responding to emails, grading papers, and preparing for the next day. She knew this situation was not sustainable; it was affecting her relationship with her husband, but she didn't know what to do. She felt guilty about "dropping" her responsibilities and thought she couldn't be an effective teacher if she did no schoolwork at home.

Sadly, this situation is not uncommon. Many teachers know that they need to take care of themselves, but they have a hard time making the time, establishing boundaries, or creating habits that support their well-being. In order for teachers to thrive in the profession for the long term, they need to "put their oxygen masks on first" and develop their resilience. Teachers who function on an empty bucket eventually burn out and leave. We need to fix that.

Indicators of Burnout

- **Emotional Exhaustion**: feelings of being emotionally overextended and exhausted by the work. Teachers may feel their emotional resources are depleted.

- **Depersonalization**: a lack of feelings for or impersonal responses toward students and colleagues. Educators may have cynical attitudes and develop a dehumanized perception of others.

- **Reduced Personal Accomplishment**: feelings of incompetence and lack of successful achievement in our work. Educators may evaluate themselves negatively and feel unhappy and dissatisfied with their accomplishments.

Source: *Maslach Burnout Inventory* by Christina Maslach, Susan E. Jackson, and Richard Schwab

The good news is that educators can avoid burnout and build their emotional strength by developing resilience—the ability to withstand stress, cope with setbacks, and overcome obstacles. Although some obstacles, such as systemic racism, discipline disparities, and inequitable outcomes for students, cannot be overcome individually, resilient educators are able to engage their optimism and focus their attention on the things that are working well, instead of solely seeing the obstacles. When teachers pay attention to their emotions and triggers, they can respond to challenging and stressful situations more intentionally. In short, resilience refers to continuing to walk toward our vision despite daily challenges, big and small.

HEART skills can help teachers develop effective strategies to deal with stressful situations and build their resilience, so they can avoid burnout and stay in the classroom for the long term.

DEVELOPING RESILIENCE USING HEART SKILLS

H—Honor Your Emotions

"What am I feeling?"

Emotions drive our behavior, and when left unchecked they can take us down a winding road. We may become reactive, live in a continuous state of stress, or feel helpless about our students. Emotions are a powerful source of information—they indicate how we interpret the various stimuli we receive from the outside world and prepare us to take action. Naming and interpreting our emotions are important steps in growing our resilience. Unless we have a sense of what we feel and why, it will be difficult to make conscious decisions about our behavior.

For example, stress is a feeling of emotional or physical tension. It can come from any situation or thought that makes us feel frustrated, worried, or angry. Stress is the way the body reacts to a challenge or difficult situation.

Think about the stress you experience at school and reflect on the following questions.

Notice: where do you feel your stress? Stress has both physical and emotional effects: headaches, irritability, lack of sleep, negative self-talk, and inability to focus. How is stress currently affecting you?

Reflect: what are the situations, circumstances, or people that are causing you stress? Write them down on a piece of paper and assign an E for Eliminate, R for Reduce, or C for Cope:

- o *E—Eliminate.* These are items that you can probably let go of. For example, if you are drowning with the never-ending to-do list, find volunteers at school (students or parents) to help you with tasks that others can do for you. They might not get done the way you would do them, but you will be able to check them off your list.

- o *R—Reduce.* Reducing the strength of the stress is sometimes a more viable solution than eliminating it entirely; for example, changing your morning or evening routine to make a better use of your time.

- o *C—Cope.* In some cases, coping might be the only option and you'll have to tap into your problem-solving skills. What are some choices given the situation? Can you look at the stressor from an alternative perspective? Who can help you?

Decide: what can you do to reduce and/or manage your stress and stressors in your life? Is there at least one thing on this list that you could try today?

- o **Focus on relationships**: Find someone in your network who can help you.

- o **Use humor:** Laugh!

- o **Exercise:** Find an activity that will get you moving. Choose something you can *realistically* incorporate into your schedule.

- o **Check-in time:** We often facilitate check-in time for our students and among staff, but what about ourselves? Did you notice how you are doing today?

- o **Create independence:** Distance yourself from unhealthy people and situations.

- o **Connect with your long-term goals:** Why do you do what you do? What keeps you going?

This simple process can help you to honor your emotions by noticing your stress and reflecting on the current stressors in your life, and then recognizing your options and deciding how you can better manage your stress today.

E—Elect your Responses

"What are my options?"

Human beings have behavior patterns that help them move through their days with ease: we commute to work, brush our teeth, or make coffee without thinking about the specific steps taken for each action. This is our brain being efficient—it doesn't use any energy, because we can do these actions almost automatically. These behavior patterns, however, are not always helpful; we often react to stressful situations automatically, without taking any time to process our feelings and think about the best way to act. We all have unproductive behaviors that seem to show up when we are tired, stressed, or distracted. We don't think, "I am going to be argumentative during the staff meeting today when they introduce the new math curriculum." It just happens, right? Or it feels that way. Choosing a different response to that situation is possible if you are able to check-in with yourself and notice your emotions.

You may learn that you are scared about this new curriculum or hurt because you were not part of the committee that made this choice. The root of your behavior may have nothing to do with the curriculum itself, but with the emotions that arise. Once you have clarity about what you feel, you can create the space to consider your options *before* taking action. But here's the thing—choice only exists if we can see it. If becoming argumentative when you are scared or hurt is a behavior pattern for you, you may not see any other options. This is where, as we have discussed, the second skill in the HEART in Mind model—Elect Your Responses—comes into place.

In the context of resilience, Elect Your Responses means being able to observe what you do when you are feeling overwhelmed or stressed by the emotional labor of teaching. Are these behaviors supporting your well-being? In what ways are these behaviors impacting others? If you realize that they are not productive, for yourself or those around you, create an alternative path by choosing a different response.

In that meeting, you may decide to name your emotions and say, "I am feeling nervous about this plan because it seems very rushed." Or you may take a few deep breaths to calm your nervous system, which will help you to better tolerate the discomfort caused by those feelings. Then, you may ask clarifying questions instead of arguing. Moving outside of your patterns can be difficult, but it is worth the effort. When you see clearly that your emotions don't need to drive your reactions, you gain freedom and more control over your life.

Electing your responses also means that you decide where to focus your attention. When we are stressed, many of us tend to pay more attention to the bad things in our lives. We may replay in our heads a challenging conversation with a student and forget how much progress our class has been making in writing. There is a scientific explanation for this. Scientists believe that we have a built-in negativity bias—our brains notice, react to, and remember negative events more than positive ones. This is because our ancestors needed to protect themselves from predators and other dangers; if they missed the threat, it could have deadly consequences— literally. According to psychologist Dr. Rick Hanson, the brain is like Velcro for negative experiences but Teflon for positive ones. This negativity bias shows up in many ways:

- In a relationship, it typically takes five good interactions to make up for a single bad one.

- People will work harder to avoid losing $100 than they will work to gain the same amount.

- Painful experiences are much more memorable than pleasurable ones.[115]

This implicit tendency toward negativity feeds many of our unpleasant emotions—worry, sorrow, anger, worthlessness—blocking the pathways for noticing the good around us. The good news is that you don't have to accept this bias. By choosing to focus your attention on the positive things happening around you, you will be able to counter your brain's tendency toward negativity. When we see the good around us, we become more resilient and able to fully experience the gift of life.

When we use this skill, Elect Your Responses, we begin by asking, "What are my options?" And this relates not only to the actions that I could take, but also to my thought patterns and the emotions that I experience. We can change the outcome of many daily situations in our lives in the classroom—and at home—when we are able to pause and create space to consider our choices before moving forward. Dr. Daniel Siegel put it this way: "Inviting our thoughts and feelings into awareness allows us to learn from them rather than be driven by them."[116]

A—Apply Empathy

"What are others feeling?"
"What would I tell a friend in the same situation?"

When I worked with neurodiverse students, I often had difficult meetings with the families. Many of these meetings occurred when a child was first identified as having special needs. In some cases, parents were upset and questioned the assessment results, believing that "the tests are biased," "they didn't provide enough information," or "the assessor doesn't even know my child." In other cases, families disagreed with the amount of specialized support built into the child's educational program. During these tense meetings, if I didn't think about how these parents felt, I became more judgmental. However, if I took the time to connect with their situation and contemplate the many emotions they could be experiencing, I felt more compassion. I felt that I wanted to work with them and support them to process this difficult situation. Empathy helps us connect with others at a deeper level.

However, applying empathy is not always easy. We are often so caught up in the situation that is difficult to see it from anybody else's point of view. We repeatedly go over *our* version of the story and justify our actions. It feels good to be right, doesn't it? This is why applying empathy in our daily lives is so important—when we ignore or undermine other people's perspectives, we are missing important information. Remember, the emotions of others are also real and it is important to validate them, even if you don't agree with them. So, when you find yourself in stressful or difficult situations, ask yourself, "What are others feeling?" Connect with those emotions and see what happens to your understanding of the issue. If anything, you will have more data to move things forward.

The other side of empathy, as we have discussed, is empathy toward oneself. I've found that this is difficult for educators. There is a shared belief that teachers are somehow super humans; they can take any amount of stress, vicarious trauma, poor working conditions, and still be a perfect role model for the children they teach. Many teachers have internalized this message and believe they are not doing enough to support children's growth and development. This is where self-compassion comes into play.

Self-compassion is not a form of indulgence; it is the ability to include the person (you) who is experiencing pain and to offer yourself some kindness. When things don't go well, it is normal to wonder why we are the center of these difficult situations. Unfortunately, often we believe that we are the only ones. Self-compassion helps us to tap into our shared humanity, recognizing that all humans experience challenging emotions many times in their lives.

I remember feeling isolated when I first moved to the United States. My English was not so great and I felt very inadequate interacting with other people. I felt, because of the language barrier, that I couldn't be myself. I spent a few weeks feeling sorry for myself and thinking that I would never fit in. Then, I decided to enroll in a conversational English class at the local adult school. I met people from Russia, Mexico, China, India, and Japan, among other places. I discovered that I was not the only one who felt inadequate—we were all trying to find our voice in this country.

It was a healing experience; I formed friendships that lasted a long time and I was able to turn around my feelings of isolation. By connecting with the difficulties of others, I was able to offer myself some compassion and was better able to navigate those challenges. Self-compassion researcher Dr. Kristin Neff reminds us that self-compassion is not another self-help approach, but a research-based strategy that supports emotional well-being and nurtures a happier and more hopeful approach to life.[117]

When you are in the midst of a challenging situation, ask yourself, "What would I tell a friend in the same situation?" You would probably share some words of encouragement, maybe invite that person to do something fun together, or maybe you would give them hug. By asking this practical question, we can apply the same kindness and compassion that we would offer others, to ourselves. We deserve it too.

R—Reignite Your Relationships

"What are my sources of strength and connection?"

Although resilience may seem like an individual effort, it is actually a community endeavor. Researchers have found that having strong personal attachments contributes to the capacity of making sense of one's life. In turn, the experience of purpose and a meaningful life enhances people's resilience and protects them against the damaging effects of major life changes.[118] This means that having strong support networks is essential to building educators' capacity to overcome challenges in healthy ways.

Some schools do a great job building structures that support strong relationships among teachers. For example, some schools use their staff meetings as a space for teachers to connect, get to know each other at a deeper level, and have educators get help and support with challenging situations. At a community high school in the San Fernando Valley, California, where I conducted a case study, staff meetings always started with appreciations. Teachers would go around the room and take a minute to acknowledge a colleague for something they did or would appreciate something that was happening at the school. This type of activity creates relational trust and a sense of comradery and belonging among staff, because it highlights teachers' positive contributions to each other and the school community while creating a space for teachers to feel seen and valued.

If your school doesn't have any structures that facilitate connection among the staff, it is even more important that you create this space for yourself. Author Elena Aguilar recommends creating a few relationship-building habits at the beginning of the school year so that teachers can build strong connections with their colleagues and be able to reach out when difficulties arise.[119] There are many ways that teachers can reach out to connect with their colleagues and learn about their lives beyond the classroom:

- Celebrate birthdays
- Attend social events
- Schedule weekly or biweekly get-togethers
- Join a committee
- Collaborate on lesson planning
- Ask for and provide feedback
- Ask for help
- Co-teach or merge classrooms for certain events

These are just some ideas to get you started. You might also begin with something small, such as eating your lunch in the staff room instead of at your desk. The goal is not to add something else to your already full to-do list, but to create opportunities for you to connect with other adults during the day.

This is also applicable to your relationships outside of school. If teaching is making you feel overwhelmed and emotionally drained, positive social relationships can serve as a protective factor—they will help you maintain better physical and emotional health and bring you joyful moments. Although research shows the many benefits of nurturing these positive relationships, we often perceive these moments as a distraction to our teaching duties. We may hesitate to visit with family or friends if we have to grade papers or plan for the following week. However, these relationships actually support our effectiveness as teachers—they help us cope with challenges and stay in the profession for the long term.

A practical question to help you create these relationship-building habits is to ask yourself, "What are my sources of strength and connection?" This is a powerful question, as it requires you to consider the people in your life that provide joy, laughter, and support. By nurturing those relationships, you are building a more resilient life.

T—Transform with Purpose

"What is my true goal?"

A few years back, I agreed to help organize an "SEL Day" at a local school. The organizing team did not seem to have a clear direction but I agreed anyway, thinking that I could be of help. As the team started making decisions about the event, I became increasingly frustrated—I thought there were better ways to present information, engage the participants, or select speakers. Since I did not want to confront the group's decisions, I became disengaged and lost interest. Then, as we were getting closer to the day of the event, I realized that I had forgotten the very reason why I had agreed to support this initiative: I wanted to support this group in pursuing something that was important to them and that aligned with my own values. My purpose was not about creating the "perfect" event according to *my* criteria, it was about supporting this group of people. When I realized that it was about them, not me, my feelings changed—I felt excited and proud of the work that had been done so far. In the end, the event was a success. Although my initial feelings were valid, I had been putting my attention on the wrong thing—I had been so focused on the outcome that I had missed the value of the process. By revisiting my purpose, I was able to see the situation from a different perspective and transform my emotions, thoughts, and the actions I took. It was a powerful reminder of what was truly important in that situation.

As we have discussed, the last skill in the HEART in Mind model, Transform with Purpose, informs our daily actions. Having clarity about our intentions and objectives makes it easier to navigate challenges and stay focused on what is really important. However, this is an intentional practice—it doesn't *just happen*. It requires that we consciously (re)visit our purpose, checking in to see if our personal interests, values, or skills have changed over time. If they have changed, we need to consider what that means for us and our work. Sometimes we need to revisit this purpose because we get caught up in different situations (trying to take control or prove we are right) and we forget our true intentions, as happened to me when I tried to help organize the SEL day.

In the context of resilience, transforming with purpose means that we use these intentions to make better, more informed, decisions and navigate the setbacks that we will inevitably encounter. A practical way to do this is by asking the question: "What is my true goal here?" This question can be applied to small situations, such as an argument with a colleague or a student, or big situations, such as considering a leadership role or changing schools. When we ask this question, we are trying to get to the core of the matter, seeing past the noise and details that make our vision blurry. Acknowledging the true value of what is happening—and bringing our purpose forward—is a process.

By engaging in this process, we can feel more grounded, resourced, and in control of our decisions. We are open to life's experiences, while feeling ready for whatever those may be.

Developing educator resilience through five HEART questions:

H	What am I feeling?
E	What are my options?
A	What are they feeling? What would I tell a friend in the same situation?
R	What are my sources of strength and connection?
T	What is my true goal?

Endnotes

115   Aguilar, Elena. *Onward: Cultivating Emotional Resilience in Educators*. Hoboken, NJ: John Wiley & Sons, 2018.

116   Martínez, Lorea, and Hannah Melnick. "Preparing Teachers to Support Social and Emotional Learning." Learning Policy Institute. May 21, 2019. https://learningpolicyinstitute.org/product/social-and-emotional-learning-case-study-san-jose-state-report.

117   Freedman, Joshua. *At The Heart of Leadership: How to Get Results with Emotional Intelligence*. Six Seconds, 2012

118   Machielse, A. "Social Isolation, Meaning-in-Life, and Resilience." *Innovation in Aging*, 2, 2018: 25.

119   Daskal, Lolly. *The Leadership Gap: What Gets Between You and Your Greatness*. New York: Portfolio, 2017.

Chapter 10: Doing the Work that Matters

"The two most important days of your life are the day you are born and the day you know why."

—*Mark Twain*

I have met many inspiring educators over the years, teachers with a commitment to contribute to their communities and change the odds for children who have been traditionally underserved by the educational system. I have also met teachers who work with middle- and upper-class students and worry about the increased anxiety and stress levels their students experience, hoping to support these students in developing healthy stress management habits and inspire them to find some enjoyment in learning. No matter where they teach, educators generally come to teaching with a strong sense of purpose.

Over time, however, teachers can become disengaged and question the value of their work or the impact they have on students. You may have experienced this yourself (or have seen your colleagues go through similar trying times) and questioned the very reason why you decided to become an educator. This is a normal and, actually, a healthy practice. Revisiting the "why" of your work can strengthen your commitment and help you move forward, even when facing difficult situations. It is important to go back to that purpose question—why does the work I do matter to me?

This is a question that may help educators prioritize their work as they deal with conflicting priorities or the endless to-do list. What happens if you give yourself permission to prioritize based on the work that is most important to you as an educator and to your students?

In a community high school in California's San Fernando Valley, the staff's shared purpose is creating a school "worthy of their own children." Their instructional program, teaching practices, and system of supports reflect this purpose. They are moved by the commitment to build a learning environment where their own kids could thrive, a school where they would be proud to send their own children. This is setting up a high standard; the teachers hold each other accountable in keeping this commitment at the forefront as they make programmatic decisions. This clear sense of purpose grounds teachers to make intentional decisions and *choose* to do their best teaching every single day.

Schools that consider and develop the HEART skills of the adults working with children know that helping teachers connect with their purpose creates a healthier and more committed community of learners. This is why more and more schools incorporate teachers' HEART growth as part of their SEL initiatives. However, if your school is not one of them, you can still take steps to bring your purpose forward in your teaching, while creating classrooms worthy of your own children.

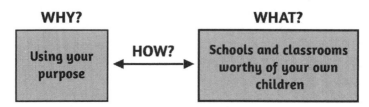

Being a whole-hearted educator means that you are focused on *doing the work that matters;* that means being grounded on your purpose, your why, in order to create schools and classrooms worthy of your own children. There are three steps that can help you move forward in accomplishing this endeavor: articulating your teaching philosophy, asserting your voice, and leading from the heart. That is doing the work that matters. The rest is noise.

ARTICULATE YOUR TEACHING PHILOSOPHY

Teachers should be able to articulate the frameworks, principles, and values that inform their teaching. Doing so is a way for educators to describe how they make decisions in the classroom and why these decisions are good for students. In the case study "Preparing Teachers to Support Social Emotional Learning," which I conducted with my colleague Hanna Melnick from the Learning Policy Institute, we studied how teacher educators at San Jose State University infused SEL in their courses.[120] One of my favorite activities in the classroom management course was the creation of a folder for a substitute teacher; teacher candidates were asked to write a letter to a substitute teacher who might teach their class on a day when they were absent. The letter needed to include the classroom's norms and procedures as well as the teacher candidate's teaching philosophy. The folder also needed to include a classroom map, in which teacher candidates had to explain how their classroom's layout supported different types of learning, such as independent or group work.

I thought this was a great activity to help teachers articulate their teaching philosophy and how it aligns with their classroom routines, norms, and space organization. For example, if teachers are passionate about developing students' independence, their classroom routines and physical space should reflect that. Or, if educators believe in using art as a vehicle for identity exploration, we should be able to see it in students' work samples.

The exercise of creating a letter to a potential substitute teacher is worth doing. Pick up a pen and a piece of paper and describe your teaching philosophy, classroom norms and routines, and student expectations. Use bullet points or drawings if they help you express yourself better. When you are done, take a few minutes to consider these questions:

- How is your teaching philosophy aligned with your norms and routines?

- Are there ways in which they are not aligned? How?

- What did you learn while doing this exercise?

- Are there any changes that you would like to implement based on this exercise?

It is fairly common to find educators who are not fully living their teaching philosophies; they may find it challenging to execute their ideas in their current school or feel it is not worth a fight with administration. It is also possible for educators to feel unsure about how to put their teaching philosophy into practice while maintaining a sense of control in their classrooms. If this is happening to you, approach it with curiosity:

- I wonder what is getting in the way of implementing my teaching philosophy.

- I wonder how my HEART skills can support me in taking one step closer to my teaching philosophy.

Engaging in this kind of reflective practice will support you in connecting with and prioritizing the things that are important to you as an educator and to your students' growth and development.

ASSERT YOUR VOICE

I will never forget the first time I watched the movie *Dead Poets Society*; I was amazed by the English teacher's capacity to inspire in his students a love for poetry and the desire to make their lives extraordinary. Considering the elite and conservative boarding school where he taught, the teacher in the film, John Keating, used some unorthodox methods. It took courage to teach what he loved and to do it in a way that truly impacted his students.

I was fortunate to have a teacher like this—my middle school social studies teacher. He taught me to love history and encouraged me to study topics of interest. He nurtured my love for learning. Also, he was not afraid of trying new things in the classroom—we took tests with a partner, had lessons outdoors, and went on field trips to interview local people. He had a way of bringing his content to life and tried hard to reach all the students in his class.

What would it take for all teachers to inspire a love for learning in their students? I believe it takes courage. As noted earlier, courage is not the absence of fear, but our ability to do something that may be scary. Its Latin root, *cor*, means heart; and in its earlier forms, the word "courage" meant, "To speak one's mind by telling all one's heart." Putting these two definitions together, we can say that being courageous means whole-heartedly taking action even when we are frightened.

In the context of teaching, being courageous might mean yielding control so we can empower our students to make decisions or form opinions on their own; it might mean focusing on the process of learning, with all its messiness, instead of the final outcome. It might also mean examining our own privilege and bias. Above all, being courageous means that you assert your voice in order to do the work that matters: Not the work that others have told you to do because there is this regulation or that standard, but the work that you know is needed to provide students with a true opportunity to grow and thrive.

Teaching is a courageous act because it requires that we face the voices—some internal, others external—that question, criticize, undermine, or block our best work. Our students need us to overcome the things that get in the way of great teaching and to conquer the fear of not knowing where we will arrive once we have departed. To do the work that matters, we cannot begin from a place of complacency or despair, but from a place of courage, confidence, and hope.

LEAD FROM THE HEART

Leaders who lead from the heart cultivate a sense of belonging, trust, and commitment within their teams, which allows every individual to bring their best work forward to accomplish great results.[121] These leaders are not necessarily those with a title (principal, director, superintendent), but those individuals who are committed to inspiring others to dream more, do more, and learn more.

It is time for educators to see themselves as leaders, not only of their students but also of the adults who work with them. Teachers may think about the impact they have on their students, but they may fail to consider the positive influence they can have on their colleagues or other adults working on campus. This is not about what title you have at school, but how you use your HEART skills, carry your purpose, and assert your voice. When teachers see themselves as leaders in this work, they can bring other teachers into the vision so that—together—the best work for students can be accomplished.

Research on SEL implementation is clear—a school-wide approach is most effective when trying to teach social and emotional skills to students.[122]However, you don't need to wait for your principal or superintendent to make this work happen; you can inspire others by sharing your own practice, supporting other teachers' efforts, and coming together as a learning community.

When you lead from the heart, you use your strengths to energize others to do more in order to support students' growth and development. While there is no formula for great leadership, effective leaders build their leadership on the following principles:[123]

- **Lead by example.** You embrace and practice your HEART skills on a regular basis. You have clarity around your purpose and teaching philosophy, and you assert your voice.

- **Lead with confidence.** You share what you know with others, you provide and ask for feedback. You are continuously learning about yourself and how to bring a HEART in Mind approach to your school.

- **Lead with humility.** You acknowledge your vulnerabilities and mistakes. You seek guidance and support. You display confidence, even when asking for help.

- **Lead with integrity.** You are honest and show a consistent adherence to strong moral and ethical principles and values. These values guide your daily actions, even when you have to make difficult decisions.

Michael Fullan, author, speaker and worldwide authority on educational reform and leadership, discusses how leadership inevitably involves trying to effect significant changes. In the case of SEL, as with other school initiatives, it will be hard for these changes to take place without changes in individual behaviors.[124] Focusing on HEART skills can help us articulate how and why we can change our individual behaviors and, in turn, help others do the same.

Throughout this book, we have reviewed several concepts—emotional triggers, empathy, importance of active listening, value of purpose—that can support teachers and administrators in exploring these changes through a shared language and framework. By embracing our HEART skills in leading change, we will be able to support ourselves and others in moving from a place of judgment, blame, and complaint to a place of curiosity, responsibility, and commitment.

When the stakeholders in the learning community create this shared commitment, great opportunities are created for children and the adults who work with them to connect, share, and become the best version of themselves.

Endnotes

120   Martínez, Lorea. "Teachers' Voices on Social Emotional Learning: Identifying the conditions that make implementation possible." PhD diss., Universitat Autònoma de Barcelona, 2013, http://hdl.handle.net/10803/378029.

121   Freedman, Joshua. At *The Heart of Leadership: How to Get Results with Emotional Intelligence*. Six Seconds, 2012.

122   Durlak, Joseph A., Celine E. Domitrovich, Roger P. Weissberg, and Thomas P. Gullotta, eds. *Handbook of Social Emotional Learning: Research and Practice*. New York, NY: Guilford Press, 2016.

123   Daskal, Lolly. *The Leadership Gap: What Gets Between You and Your Greatness*. New York: Portfolio, 2017.

124   Fullan, Michael. *Leadership & Sustainability: System Thinkers in Action*. Thousand Oaks, CA: Corwin, 2004.

PART 4: PUTTING ALL THE PIECES TOGETHER

Chapter 11: Teaching and Learning with the HEART in Mind

In a fast-paced and changing world, children need tools to be able to face failure and disappointment, work in teams, and be adaptable, just as much as they need to know algebra and the economic implications of World War II. Choosing between academics and SEL is a false dichotomy—students need to be academically prepared as well as socially and emotionally equipped. SEL, with the practical application of the HEART in Mind model, has the potential to create classrooms where students can engage with academic content in deeper ways, learn and value their classmates, and find ways to contribute to their communities. SEL is not a new fad in education reform, but a new paradigm in teaching and learning and an essential tool for creating caring, committed citizens and thriving communities.

Teaching with the HEART in Mind is based on the premise that it is possible and necessary to help teachers build practices that address the whole child, integrating both the cognitive and social-emotional development of children. The HEART in Mind model offers educators a framework for teaching and practicing social and emotional skills, while analyzing and refining their teaching with an SEL lens. When teachers engage in this process, they are better able to understand and communicate with students, feel empowered to "stop instructional time" to address classroom issues, and have more tools for responding to students' needs.[125] By putting into practice the tools and strategies that we have explored in this book, teachers can build their resilience and that of their students, so we can collectively act to overcome the challenges of our times—the systemic racism, the inequitable impact of a global pandemic, the deficit-based mindsets of our educational system. However, creating these positive outcomes calls for teachers to do one thing—to try.

PRACTICE COUNTS

Findings from my doctoral dissertation provided some evidence that the *experience* of teaching SEL has a positive influence in teachers' pedagogical thinking about SEL. When teachers continuously implement SEL programs and practices, they develop their SEL pedagogy and deepen their commitment to the whole child.

At the same time, when teachers adopt a "learn by doing" mindset in the implementation process, they are better able to see themselves as learners, opening the door for collaboration with the staff and able to support each other as challenges arise.

CHALLENGES CAN BE PRODUCTIVE

You will most likely face challenges and roadblocks when you adopt the HEART in Mind model in your classroom and school. These can be internal (feeling insecure, not scheduling SEL time, struggling to change habits) or external (lack of resources, administrative support, or staff commitment) and they are normal.

The challenges don't need to be "deal breakers" in your SEL implementation process; some of them may actually help you and your school strengthen the vision, bring people together, or better plan for the future. Therefore, accept the difficulties as necessary steps in the process.

- *Time constraints*. Time is a precious resource in schools; we never seem to have enough time to do everything we would like and are asked to do. When it comes to SEL, teachers may find it difficult to incorporate explicit instruction of HEART skills in their schedule or follow a scope and sequence.

Tips: While it may seem easier to skip your SEL lesson when you are behind with other academic units, the truth is that helping students develop these skills and creating a cohesive environment in the classroom will support students' learning of other skills and content. If you do need extra time, omit one or two activities, but don't skip your SEL time altogether.

- *Need for differentiation.* No matter how well you use the strategies suggested in this book or the lessons you create yourself, you'll probably have to differentiate and modify, based on students' needs.

Tips: Accept the need for differentiation as an ongoing process. It will be hard to differentiate every activity when you first start teaching SEL, but over time you will learn what fits well with your voice, your students' needs, and the classroom environment.

- *Need for professional development.* In order to do this work effectively, teachers need support in developing their HEART skills and adopting SEL practices in their classroom.

Tips: Bring Teaching with the HEART in Mind to your school for a half or full day of training or join the online community forum to ask questions, share resources, and celebrate successes. Technology has made it a lot easier for teachers to create online learning communities. Make sure you access all the current resources at teachingheartinmind.com.

IT STARTS WITH YOU

There are many ways for you to teach with the HEART in Mind—starting with yourself—by practicing and modeling these important skills, extending them to your students, and creating a caring, trusting, and equitable learning environment. There will be days when it feels like you have not made any progress. I know I have said this before, but it is all part of the process. When this happens, you start again. One step at a time, moving forward to nurture yourself and create a community where children and youth can thrive and be prepared for the future.

While there are numerous school initiatives that aim to teach students the necessary skills to be college and career ready, SEL is the only one that supports children and youth in finding the inner strength to drive their own learning and become the best versions of themselves. Embracing HEART skills matters because it asks every person working with kids to be fully human and to reclaim the humanity of our children and youth.

If we want to change the odds for children, we must make a different choice. I invite you wholeheartedly to walk with me with courage and confidence to create a better future for ourselves and our children. You hold the power—choose to teach with the HEART in Mind!

Endnotes

125   Martínez, Lorea. "Teachers' Voices on Social Emotional Learning: Identifying the conditions that make implementation possible." PhD diss., Universitat Autònoma de Barcelona, 2013, http://hdl.handle.net/10803/378029.

Appendix

HEART SKILLS SCOPE AND SEQUENCE

This tool is available for download at loreamartinez.com.

Honor Your Emotions

Beginner	Advanced Beginner	Strategic Learner	Emerging Expert	Practicing Expert
Uses a variety of emotion words.	Describes a range of emotions.	Recognizes the different degrees of intensity in their emotions.	Analyzes factors that create difficult emotions, such as stress or fear.	Identifies how emotions affect decision-making and interprets their meaning.
Connects emotions with bodily sensations.	Identifies the reasons behind their emotions.	Identifies the complexity and meaning of feelings.	Generates ways to interpret and communicate emotions.	Evaluates how expressing emotions affects others and communicates accordingly.
Describes how emotions are linked to behavior	Expresses how they feel to others.	Demonstrates when and how feelings can be communicated appropriately.	Applies strategies to use emotions effectively.	Generates ways to use emotions to accomplish personal goals.

Elect Your Responses

Beginner	Advanced Beginner	Strategic Learner	Emerging Expert	Practicing Expert
Identifies tools to manage strong emotions.	Uses self-management tools to manage emotions.	Demonstrates behavior and emotion management to maintain focus and concentration.	Demonstrates capacity to manage behavior and emotions to maintain focus on one's goals.	Adjusts behavior and emotions in response to changes in the environment or to changes in one's goals.
Describes behavior patterns.	Recognizes own typical reactions to daily situations.	Explains own patterns and things that trigger certain emotions and behaviors.	Anticipates patterns and articulates tools to change unproductive behaviors.	Uses tools and strategies to transform unproductive patterns.
Identifies challenges in daily situations.	Demonstrates reframing skills in challenging situations.	Analyzes why one achieved or did not achieve a goal.	Identifies the role of attitude and self-talk in success.	Generates alternative solutions to problems and sustains optimism.
		Uses reframing skills in daily situations.	Applies strategies to cope with a variety of stresses.	

Apply Empathy

Beginner	Advanced Beginner	Strategic Learner	Emerging Expert	Practicing Expert
Describes how others feel based on body and facial expressions.	Describes the expressed feelings and perspectives of others.	Predicts others' feelings and perspectives and explains the reasons.	Analyzes similarities and differences between one's own emotions and perspectives and those of others.	Demonstrates understanding of those who have different emotions and perspectives.
Recognizes that others may experience different emotions from oneself in similar situations.	Identifies own feelings when others are in difficult situations.	Analyzes how one's behavior may affect others.	Identifies ways to act with compassion in the community.	Demonstrates ways to act and live with compassion.
Differentiates between positive and negative self-talk.	Identifies negative self-talk in everyday situations.	Identifies and explains how negative self-talk can impact performance and well-being.	Applies strategies to reframe negative self-talk.	Generates strategies to nurture self-compassion in daily life.

Reignite Your Relationships

Beginner	Advanced Beginner	Strategic Learner	Emerging Expert	Practicing Expert
Communicates needs and wants, takes turns, and pays attention when others are speaking.	Uses active listening skills and disagrees with others in constructive ways.	Analyzes the power of one's own words to hurt and/or support others.	Analyzes effective communication strategies and uses them based on personal needs and context.	Uses assertive communication to meet needs, without negatively impacting others.
Identifies common conflicts with peers, and ways to resolve them.	Describes causes and consequences of conflicts and uses some strategies to resolve them.	Defines unhealthy peer pressure and uses skills to resolve interpersonal conflicts.	Analyzes how conflict resolution skills contribute to collaborative work and uses them effectively.	Evaluates effectiveness of one's own conflict resolution skills and plans how to improve them.
Contributes to group projects.	Analyzes ways to work in diverse groups effectively.	Demonstrates social skills when working in groups.	Evaluates one's own contributions in groups, as a member and a leader, with a racial lens.	Plans, implements, and leads participation in group projects.
Understands and appreciates diversity.	Identifies differences in the understanding of cultural norms.	Develops cultural awareness when establishing relationships.	Analyzes how power and privilege influence social dynamics.	Uses cultural competence and humility in building constructive relationships.

Transform with Purpose

Beginner	Advanced Beginner	Strategic Learner	Emerging Expert	Practicing Expert
Describes personal likes, dislikes, and things that are important.	Describes personal interests, skills, and values.	Analyzes how personal interests and values influence behavior and outcomes.	Articulates ways to use personal values, interests, and skills to contribute to others.	Applies personal interests, values, and strengths to contribute to others.
Identifies assets, problems, and needs at school and in the community.	Examines community assets, and identifies problems and possible solutions.	Identifies local and global community assets, problems, and their root causes.	Evaluates how systemic problems impact academic, social, and financial outcomes.	Analyzes social, economic, and political structures that maintain inequities, and acts to dismantle them.
Identifies steps to address community issues and needs.	Performs roles that contribute to improving school or the community.	Works with community members to address community issues.	Cocreates a plan to address a community issue with community members, using personal strengths.	Monitors progress toward equitable outcomes and living purposefully.

SELF-ASSESSMENT FOR ADULT HEART SKILLS

This tool is designed for self-reflection. The goal is to identify areas where you are applying your HEART skills and consider if these are strengths for you. As you reflect on the results, you might identify skills that you are not applying as intentionally. Are these challenges for you? If they are, consider choosing one or two statements that you'd like to develop. Then, list one or two things that you can do to start using that skill. This self-assessment tool is available for download at loreamartinez.com.

Honor Your Emotions

	Rarely	Sometimes	Often
I am able to identify, name, and interpret my emotions in the moment.			
I can identify how my emotions affect my decision-making process.			
I can anticipate how expressing my emotions may impact others.			
I know when and how to communicate my emotions, depending on the context and situation.			
I can use my emotions to accomplish my personal goals.			

Elect Your Responses

	Rarely	Sometimes	Often
I can adjust my behavior and emotions in response to changes in the environment.			
I can recognize my patterns and use tools to change the ones that are unproductive.			
I use tools to navigate stress, failure, and setbacks in positive ways.			
I can generate alternative solutions to problems.			
I can create and sustain optimism.			

Apply Empathy

	Rarely	Sometimes	Often
I show understanding of those who have different emotions and perspectives.			
I can feel what others feel.			
I act with compassion.			
I apply strategies to reframe negative self-talk			
I provide myself with self-care and self-compassion.			

Reignite Your Relationships

	Rarely	Sometimes	Often
I can communicate assertively and constructively.			
I practice active listening.			
I can solve conflicts and negotiate different situations successfully.			
I am trustworthy.			
I can work with diverse individuals and groups to accomplish shared goals.			

Transform with Purpose

	Rarely	Sometimes	Often
I monitor changes in my personal interests and values.			
I use my strengths to positively contribute to others.			
I actively contribute to my community.			
I understand systemic problems and act to dismantle them.			
I seek equitable outcomes for all and live a purposeful life.			

Acknowledgments

Teaching with the HEART in Mind is a book inspired by the many experiences and people that have shaped my identity as an educator and scholar. This book combines my love for teaching with purpose, social and emotional learning (SEL), excellence and equity, and a commitment to create better outcomes for children. I hope that this will be an important contribution to educators who are working hard to teach wholeheartedly in service of all children.

I thank all the students, teachers, principals, and parents who have contributed to my growth and continue to inspire me to do a job that I love. Among my colleagues I would especially like to thank my partner teacher Toni Díaz at CEIP Costa i Llobera in Barcelona, where I started my teaching career, and my friends—Josh Freedman, Dr. Anabel Jensen, Ilaria Boffa, Michael Eatman, and many others—at Six Seconds, where I found a tribe of like-minded and purposeful individuals. Another special thank you goes to Dr. Susan Stillman, mentor and dear friend, who encouraged me to pursue a career focused on SEL and has rooted for me through ups and downs.

I am grateful to my mentor, Dr. Miquel Àngel Essomba from the Universitat Autònoma de Barcelona, for guiding me to pursue a doctoral program which would lead me to find my passion for SEL. And thank you to Dr. Rafael

Bisquerra both for the many contributions to the SEL field in Spain and internationally and for inspiring me to advance this work in the United States.

Thank you to Dr. Brian Perkins and my students and colleagues at Teachers College, Columbia University, for giving me the opportunity to teach and learn together. Their commitment and integrity help me move forward despite the current challenges. A special appreciation goes to Dr. Yvette Jackson, who has become a guiding light in my journey. I am honored to have your wisdom in the foreword of this book. And thank you to my research colleagues at the Learning Policy Institute, for their rigor and commitment to excellence.

I extend my appreciation to David Rust and the learning team at the Hispanic Information and Telecommunications Network (HITN) for believing in this work and inviting me to become a partner in their mission to support Hispanic and Latino families. My commitment to helping those who have been underserved by the educational system has been strengthened because of your work.

My deepest gratitude to my book reviewers—Dr. Tia Barnes, Dr. Deborah Donahue-Keegan, Dr. Yvette Jackson, Maricela Montoy-Wilson, Dr. Susan Stillman, and Dr. Shannon Wanless. They not only provided brilliant suggestions, but also filled me with their encouragement and support. Any errors remain mine.

Thank you to the team that made this project come into fruition through editing, project management, and publishing guidance—Julie Broad, Jaqueline Kyle, Melissa Sobey, Kelly Ragan, Judith Cressy, and many others who worked behind the scenes. A special thank you goes to Alissa Looney, who worked her magic to create compelling images.

And finally, I thank my family and friends for their unconditional love and support. To my parents, Rafi and Benito, *gracias por enseñarme tantas cosas*, and to my sister Noelia and her family, for rooting me on throughout this entire process. I am grateful to my abuelita Teresa, who I know is looking after me from heaven. I thank Edgar and Irene for being there, no matter the time. To *mis niñas bonitas*, Teresa and Clara, for lifting me up with your love, laughter, and silliness. And to my loving husband, John Rethans, for not letting me give up on this dream.

Made in the USA
Coppell, TX
21 February 2021